Cambridge Elements

Elements in Critical Heritage Studies
edited by
Kristian Kristiansen
University of Gothenburg
Michael Rowlands
UCL

AI AND IMAGE

Critical Perspectives on the Application of Technology on Art and Cultural Heritage

Anna Foka
Uppsala University

Jan von Bonsdorff
Uppsala University

Shaftesbury Road, Cambridge CB2 8EA, United Kingdom

One Liberty Plaza, 20th Floor, New York, NY 10006, USA

477 Williamstown Road, Port Melbourne, VIC 3207, Australia

314–321, 3rd Floor, Plot 3, Splendor Forum, Jasola District Centre, New Delhi – 110025, India

103 Penang Road, #05–06/07, Visioncrest Commercial, Singapore 238467

Cambridge University Press is part of Cambridge University Press & Assessment, a department of the University of Cambridge.

We share the University's mission to contribute to society through the pursuit of education, learning and research at the highest international levels of excellence.

www.cambridge.org
Information on this title: www.cambridge.org/9781009505482

DOI: 10.1017/9781009505468

© Anna Foka and Jan von Bonsdorff 2025

This publication is in copyright. Subject to statutory exception and to the provisions of relevant collective licensing agreements, with the exception of the Creative Commons version the link for which is provided below, no reproduction of any part may take place without the written permission of Cambridge University Press & Assessment.

An online version of this work is published at doi.org/10.1017/9781009505468 under a Creative Commons Open Access license CC-BY-NC 4.0 which permits re-use, distribution and reproduction in any medium for non-commercial purposes providing appropriate credit to the original work is given and any changes made are indicated. To view a copy of this license visit https://creativecommons.org/licenses/by-nc/4.0

When citing this work, please include a reference to the DOI 10.1017/9781009505468

First published 2025

A catalogue record for this publication is available from the British Library

ISBN 978-1-009-50548-2 Hardback
ISBN 978-1-009-50549-9 Paperback
ISSN 2632-7074 (online)
ISSN 2632-7066 (print)

Cambridge University Press & Assessment has no responsibility for the persistence or accuracy of URLs for external or third-party internet websites referred to in this publication and does not guarantee that any content on such websites is, or will remain, accurate or appropriate.

For EU product safety concerns, contact us at Calle de José Abascal, 56, 1°, 28003 Madrid, Spain, or email eugpsr@cambridge.org

AI and Image

Critical Perspectives on the Application of Technology on Art and Cultural Heritage

Elements in Critical Heritage Studies

DOI: 10.1017/9781009505468
First published online: September 2025

Anna Foka
Uppsala University

Jan von Bonsdorff
Uppsala University

Author for correspondence: Anna Foka, anna.foka@abm.uu.se

Abstract: *AI and Image* illustrates the importance of critical perspectives in the study of AI and its application to image collections in the art and heritage sector. The authors' approach is that such entanglements of image and AI are neither dystopian nor utopian but may amplify, reduce, or condense existing societal inequalities depending on how they may be implemented in relation to human expertise and sensibility in terms of diversity and inclusion. The Element further discusses regulations around the use of AI for such cultural datasets as they touch upon legalities, regulations, and ethics. In the conclusion they emphasise the importance of the professional expert factor in the entanglements of AI and images and advocate for a continuous and renegotiating professional symbiosis between human and machines. This title is also available as Open Access on Cambridge Core.

Keywords: artificial intelligence, art, art history, cultural heritage, humanities

© Anna Foka and Jan von Bonsdorff 2025

ISBNs: 9781009505482 (HB), 9781009505499 (PB), 9781009505468 (OC)
ISSNs: 2632-7074 (online), 2632-7066 (print)

Contents

1 Introduction: AI and the Art and Cultural Heritage Image: Visual Literacy and Machine Learning   1

2 Current Trends on AI and Art and Culture   19

3 Dystopian or Utopian Futures?   41

4 Harnessing Machines: Cultural Policy, Participation, and Implementation   61

5 Conclusions and Prospects for the Future of AI in Art and Culture   67

  Glossary   75

  References   77

1 Introduction: AI and the Art and Cultural Heritage Image: Visual Literacy and Machine Learning

1.1 About This Element

1.1.1 This Element's aims and objectives

Over the past three decades, galleries, libraries, archives, and museums (GLAM) have undergone profound digital transformation. Collections of sketches, photographs, paintings, and maps are turning rapidly into datasets, enriched with structured machine-readable descriptions or metadata. In the same breath, new datasets are being 'born' in entirely digital formats, such as memes, synthetic art, and comics. Millions of images are owned and classified by different GLAM stakeholders every day, such as Amsterdam's Rjksmuseum or Getty Images. While we are used to trained experts, humans are using their best judgement to manage, to curate, and to classify images and image datasets, yet machines, that is, computers in general, have become increasingly influential in assisting or even performing these tasks. Within the cultural and creative sectors, the implementation of artificial intelligence (AI) methods is a rapidly growing area of interest, specifically in relation to images and pictorial collections. On the one hand, as AI is a wide field of inquiry, research methods and implementation may vary significantly and seem to have enormous potential. On the other hand, given the diversity of contexts of human representation, memory, and culture, the complexity of open access, the lack of funding, and its very impact on climate change, AI has been approached with caution. In this Element we hope to provide a thorough analysis of this polarity, while highlighting how AI may be of effective assistance to professionals in the GLAM sector.

1.1.2 Some Terminologies and a Short State-of-the-Art

AI has become a broad term encompassing a variety of technologies, tools, and methods that support and enable information processing and decision-making beyond human intervention. *Machine learning* is a subset of AI where algorithms learn from data to make predictions or decisions without explicit programming (see Figure 5). Another way to describe this is that AI is an intelligent behaviour that can be achieved using machine learning. Naturally, as this is an Element dealing with AI and Image, computer vision is central to this Element. *Computer vision* is the scientific and technological discipline involving processing and understanding images. Computer vision serves as the foundational technology that explores and advances computer capabilities at a general level, whereas *machine vision* applies these technologies specifically to optimise industrial operations. Throughout this Element we refer to computer vision to

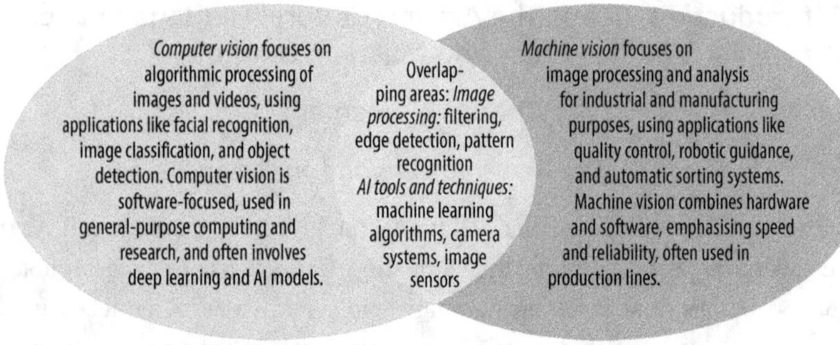

Computer vision focuses on algorithmic processing of images and videos, using applications like facial recognition, image classification, and object detection. Computer vision is software-focused, used in general-purpose computing and research, and often involves deep learning and AI models.

Overlapping areas: *Image processing:* filtering, edge detection, pattern recognition. *AI tools and techniques:* machine learning algorithms, camera systems, image sensors.

Machine vision focuses on image processing and analysis for industrial and manufacturing purposes, using applications like quality control, robotic guidance, and automatic sorting systems. Machine vision combines hardware and software, emphasising speed and reliability, often used in production lines.

Figure 1 The distinctions and overlaps between computer vision and machine vision. Computer vision (left) focuses on algorithmic processing of images for applications like facial recognition and object detection, primarily in software-driven environments. Machine vision (right) is tailored for industrial and manufacturing purposes. The overlapping area highlights shared techniques such as image processing and the use of AI tools, which are central to both fields. Illustration: J. v. Bonsdorff.

describe the technology, and machine vision is used in a more general context (see Figure 1). Machine vision is most beneficial for tasks requiring precision and consistency, typically in the context of digitisation and conservation workflows. In contrast, computer vision is key to the interpretative, analytical, and public-facing aspects of cultural heritage, offering tools to enhance understanding of cultural assets. In this Element, we concentrate on the latter, that is, computer vision. *Generative AI* is a type of artificial intelligence that creates new content, such as text, images, videos, audio, and synthetic data, using generative models. These models learn patterns and structures from their training data and generate new data with similar characteristics in response to prompts (cf. Section 2.2.3).

Recent research attempts to refine models of practice particularly concerning the application of AI methods and tools in datasets but also the legal parameters such as ownership and copyright, as well as ethics. AI for cultural heritage collections remains a novelty even in countries like our native Sweden, where digitisation has a long tradition and legacy, due to lack of expertise and funding models for lifelong learning education for professionals (Griffin et al., 2023). Yet worldwide it is globally considered a curation management support in creative and effective ways (Ciecko, 2020). There are fewer critical reflections on historical image collections and AI. An exception is the edited volume by Bordoni et al. (2016) on AI innovation within the cultural heritage sector from the perspectives of cultural history, semantic digital archives, the use of analytic tools to support visitor interpretation, augmented reality, and robotics. As such, Bordoni's edited volume is valuable yet limited to specific case studies that were published in 2016, and since then, technological progress brings even more possibilities which we hereby seek to address. In a similar vein there are specific articles that deal with AI and image analysis, but these are limited to certain case studies and, as such, they tend to focus on implementing technology on one type of image (e.g. handwritten archives, photography, paintings, and so on) and then discuss statistics in success rates. Other significant theoretical attempts to analyse the potential and challenges that AI technology brings into the table include Bell's work on computer vision as an art-historical tool (Bell, 2022; Bell & Ommer, 2016). In a similar vein Wright and Ommer (2021) have discussed uses of generative AI, art history, and machine vision. Thiel and Bernhard's more recent anthology (2023) provides valuable reflections on AI in museums, artistic practice, curation tools, visitor analytics, chatbots, automatic translations, and tailor-made text generation, including critical reflections, practical perspectives, and applications.

Research on AI and image normally relies on specific datasets as case studies, which may help inspire other research (see for example Karterouli et al., 2021). The types of AI and machine learning tools and practices addressed in these case studies as such include computer vision and Natural Language Processing (NLP), and also processes and tools for personalising visitor experiences. Computer vision acts through auto-generating a description or tags to make images more discoverable (Fontanella, 2020: 23–29). Giugliano and Laudante (2020) argue that technological design offers a key opportunity for the cultural heritage sector to connect technology and context in ways that transcend physical boundaries. While Giugliano and Laudante's study is focused on users, the authors argue for an expanded consideration of different stakeholders. Not only could this promote 'an increasingly wide and diversified public', they write, but technology affords opportunities to materialise a common meeting ground, a space that allows for interchange around what is shareable, accessible, and consultable (2020: 7). Existing books about AI in the arts and humanities focus on machine learning and computer vision, primarily in relation to art and creativity (Manovich and Arielli, 2024), art, machine learning and the notion of computational formalism (coined by Wasielewski, 2023a), or machine vision and its applications more generally (Rettberg, 2023).

As it transpires from this short state of the art, traditions for AI implementation in museums and heritage organisations vary greatly, encompassing concepts of reasoning, classification, knowledge representation, curation, or learning and dissemination, utilising image processing and analysis. Recent research has challenged and refined models of practice in this domain. There is a growing use and interest of AI in museums, where they collaborate with industry partners to harness AI for collections management in creative and effective ways. Critical engagement with AI technologies and their potential for museums is a focus of attention of this Element. *AI and Image* essentially explores how AI may contribute in staging and curating image collections through automated processes and machine learning. Like Gartski (2020), we seek to chart the way professionals and practitioners in the last two decades have worked to integrate a wide range of emerging AI tools and methods to enhance the curation, analysis, and dissemination of image datasets. As with archaeology, AI methods and tools have expanded and altered the landscape of art and culture. At the same time *AI and Image* critically assesses AI and outlines possibilities and complexity within the disciplines of art and heritage studies as well as in the praxis of cultural heritage preservation and public engagement. We begin in Section 1 from the basics, essentially defining what is an image, explaining concepts of visual literacy, and discussing even computer vision, and then in Section 2, we chart the AI technologies that have been or are currently trending in the cultural and creative sectors.

In Section 3, *AI and Image* additionally seeks to remedy the lack of critical perspectives in the study of AI and its application to image collections. The practices by which AI is given meaning and used by different segments of society may have both ontological and relational qualities embedded in the technology which need to be addressed. Currently, the application of AI seems to be amplifying societal bias especially in the context of recommender systems for heritage and art such as Google Arts and Culture, for example (Kizhner et al., 2021: 607–640). We aim at focusing on potentials and challenges in Section 3. We discuss that while AI may reinforce bias, it may also be used to reduce bias and to support cultural revitalization. Essentially, to paraphrase the work of Miller and Haapio-Kirk on *Making Things Matter* (2020) we place emphasis on the contexts and the materiality of images, their AI-driven trajectories but also on understanding why images are important to people in a world of fast-developing technologies. Thus, our approach is that such entanglements of image and AI are neither dystopian nor utopian but may amplify, reduce, or condense existing societal inequalities depending on how they may be implemented in relation to human expertise and sensibility in terms of diversity and inclusion. Section 4 assesses the regulations around the use of AI for such cultural datasets as we touch upon legalities, regulations, and ethics. In the conclusion we emphasise the importance of the professional expert factor in the entanglements of AI and images and advocate for a continuous and renegotiating professional symbiosis between human and machines.

Moving beyond case studies or professional approaches to AI in the GLAM sector, in this Element we aim at suggesting visions for the future, as well as ways towards best practice, as we envision the future potential of AI/ML. As the authors of this Element we feel we need to address that the literature mentioned in this Element primarily derives from European, British and North American case studies and practical implementation (Foka et al., 2023). We are aware, at the time of writing this Element, that the most advanced AI technologies are trending globally, with China, Singapore, Israel, South Korea, Japan, and India among the leading countries in the development. We therefore need to stress that this inquiry is relevant at a global scale and should not be limited solely to research in languages that we, authors of this Element, can read.

Last, but certainly not least, we hope to contribute to the discourse of digital transformation in historical disciplines as seen in the Cambridge Elements by Milligan, I. (2022) that all aspects of the historian's research workflow, and in our case professionals and scholars in arts and culture, have been transformed by technology. With *AI and Image* we aim at helping practitioners to experiment with these tools as well as to envisage their long-term impact.

1.2 Introduction: Humans, AI, and Image

1.2.1 Visual Literacy as a Concept: From Human to Machine/Computer Vision

In the early 2020s a Drakeposting meme (i.e. a humorous image including the R&B singer Drake) about humanity became viral on social media. It featured Drake on two poses, one approving and one disapproving, as an answer to the question of 'what makes one human'. The disapproving gesture was accompanied by the text: to love and to care for others, whereas the answer of 'selecting all images with traffic lights' featured Drake's gesticulating approval. The Drakeposting meme about reCAPTCHA systems cleverly juxtaposes humanity in the digital age. By contrasting the noble ideal of loving and caring for others with the mundane, automated task of selecting traffic light images, the meme highlights taps into the collective experience of navigating online spaces, where our humanity is often reduced to proving we are not machines through a reCAPTCHA challenge (see Drakeposting meme on CAPTCHA systems, publicly available at https://imgflip.com/i/6gk9i9).

The meme's popularity reflects a shared frustration and amusement at how our human identity is increasingly validated by our ability to perform tasks that AI struggles with, rather than by our capacity for empathy and connection. The meme's underlying commentary extends beyond mere humour, touching on profound questions about the nature of humanity in an AI-driven world. It underscores how our interactions with technology are reshaping our self-perception and societal values. The irony that selecting images of traffic lights is deemed more human than expressing love and care speaks volumes about the digital age's impact on humanity and society. This meme serves as a cultural artefact, encapsulating the complex relationship between images, humans, and AI. It reflects our growing awareness of how our online actions contribute to AI development, often unknowingly training algorithms through our responses to these challenges. This realization prompts us to consider our role as humans in shaping future AI capabilities.

How are images understood by both humans and machines? This is precisely the question that this section seeks to problematise. We begin by introducing image as a concept: how images function in human discourse and communication. In doing so we simultaneously assess how machines are taught to see, again by human intervention, but also how machines learn how to see, by training, over time. In attempting to answer the question, inevitably two further questions arise: Do we all see the same things – and by extension, do all machines see the same things or features in an image? In what follows, we go on to develop the concept of visual literacy in terms of both human and computer vision as well as discuss the implementation of artificial intelligence when it concerns image data, particularly in relation to description and classification.

One way of understanding visual content is encapsulated in the concept of visual literacy which extends beyond visual interpretation. Visual literacy refers to the quotidian competence of understanding and acting upon everyday visual cues as traffic signs, advertisements, fashion, comics, and other such visual cues. There are certainly pictorial conventions in visual cues as such; these may be dictated by time, culture, space, and overall context. The cultural codes of body language, mimics, and gestures are some examples. Visual literacy is not merely an innate trait but rather a culturally embedded and trainable skill (Johannesson, 1991). The origins of visual literacy as a concept can be found in the 1960s writings of Debes, and the Rochester School. Michelson summarises Debes's key ideas: the growing importance of analysing and documenting images, the impact of new technologies on childhood development necessitating novel educational methods, and the need for more active student engagement in learning. These concepts have remained influential regardless of their effectiveness (Michelson, 2017). The term 'visual literacy' has been further developed by a Swedish scholar (as *seendekompetens:* Johannesson, 1991, 1999): Visual literacy is something that most people possess from a very early stage of cognitive development. Johannesson points out that this well-trained visual skill is not an art-schooled way of seeing but the everyday competence acquired through social instructions seen in, for example, traffic signs, newspapers, TV programmes, car models, the signals and variations of fashion, and above all through the knowledge of the cultural codes of body language: 'We refer to visual experience as a medium through which we mould our persona, either through acceptance or struggle' (our own translation of Johannesson, 1991: 11). Here, we use the concept of visual literacy mainly in two capacities: First, as an innate competence of the general gallery museum public, which can be developed through educational means. Second, as the rich trove of meaning-carrying pictorial conventions that have accumulated through the centuries – and may be of use in how humans may train machines.

But if there is visual literacy for humans, is there a visual literacy of sorts for machines? Jill Walker Rettberg in her book *Machine Vision* begins by describing how human vision and machine vision are intrinsically similar and different (Rettberg, 2023: 1–24). Human vision is articulated as this limited perspective that aims straight ahead – no peripheral vision, no ultraviolet light, for example. Technology, on the other hand, has been augmenting human vision, enabling us to see differently and to see more. However, precisely as with human vision, machine vision comes with restraints and complexity (Rettberg, 2023: 2). While Rettberg chooses the term 'machine vision' to incorporate visual technologies that precede artificial intelligence, computer vision and machine vision are to some extent used interchangeably at a global scale, to discuss technologies that aim at helping us humans to see, or helping us to classify and to describe visual aids, beyond our eyesight alone (see Figure 1). In this context of machine vision as a tool, Bell (2022: 392 f.) speaks about a *structured seeing* (in German: *strukturiertes Sehen*), based on more visual parameters that may break but, at the same time, add to linear classification systems like traditional lists or catalogues. In this light, human vision comes with a combination of our senses and their interpretation by our human brain; a combination of contexts, knowledge, and further cognition aids our interpretation. The process with computers and machines is slightly different – but yet trained initially by our human perception. The relationship between human and machine vision underscores the need to approach visual literacy not merely as a passive reception of images but as an active engagement with the *cultural, social, and epistemological* dimensions of the image. Visual literacy can therefore be analysed, described, and taught to humans and machines alike.

1.2.2 What Is an Image, and How We Define It throughout This Element

> As goodness stands in the intelligible realm to intelligence and the things we know,
> *so does the sun stand in the visible realm to sight and the things we see.*
> – Plato, *Republic* 6:508 c, authors' own translation

The proverb 'an image speaks volumes' implies, according to the Cambridge Dictionary, that an image may make an opinion, characteristic, or situation very clear without the use of words. We cannot deny the power of images and how they are imbued with meaning. We can further not deny their historical uses over centuries. The importance of image descriptions, analogies, and metaphors has been present since the beginning of time. In Homer, cities and communities are often likened to ships in powerful visual analogies. The Greek philosopher Plato discusses the image as unable to be 'the truth'. However, the very same Plato places images at the core of his philosophical analysis. Platonic descriptions of images, often discussed as analogies, are used to describe complex philosophical phenomena. These Platonic image-analogies are commonly understood as illustrations of arguments. Paradoxically, in *Analogy of the Sun*, in Plato's *Republic*, Socrates compares *the Good* with the Sun. Plato might be using the image of the Sun to help bring life to his arguments or to make the argument more clearly understood. Platonic images as such occur often, but they are based on the prominence of the pictured objects themselves. Images are depictions, symbols, interpretations. As such they reflect these precise Platonist frames of thought: the *noumenal* and the *phenomenal*. The noumenal, that is, the world known by intellect, is considered superior to the phenomenal realm, the material, physical world of immediate sensory perception, vision, hearing, experience. Experiencing, and in this particular case 'seeing', images provides an initiating act towards examination, analysis, and scholarly reflection. Similar to the rhetorical device of *ekphrasis*, which may be used to describe a work of art, a description of an image, even as a rhetorical or philosophical device, provides humans with a paroxysm of meanings, masked as symbols, providing contexts, concepts, and uses. As such, reality has always been interpreted by reports given by images (Sontag, 1977a: 153–156). Images thus are pregnant with information that our minds interpret accordingly.

We follow W. J. T. Mitchell in defining the image incorporating any visual likeness, figure, motif, or form that appears in a medium (Mitchell, 2005: xiii) as well as Hans Belting's anthropological notion of the image: Belting adds the 'body' framing the image together with the medium (Belting, 2005: 302). The image does not appear solely in the medium or in the body but in the interplay between the two: thus, we understand the term 'image' as encompassing a wide range of meanings, including a physical likeness or representation of a person, animal, or thing that can be photographed, painted, sculptured, or otherwise made visible. It may simultaneously refer to a mental picture or idea of something in one's mind, the way a person, group, or organisation appears to others, often deliberately created or modified by publicity, advertising, propaganda, and so on, and a poetic description of something. An image can be a symbol, emblem, or a type that embodies a particular quality or concept. Throughout this Element, we further stress the material aspects of the image, the

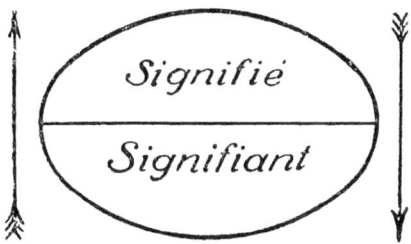

Figure 2 A generic diagram from Ferdinand de Saussure's Cours de linguistique générale illustrating the relationship between signified (French Signifié) and signifier (French Signifiant). Ferdinand de Saussure, Cours de linguistique générale, Paris 1922 (2nd ed.), p. 158.

image as a material entity – as is the traditional approach within a European cultural heritage context that values matter, material, and its preservation/conservation.

We further understand images as signs, illuminating their duality: their material attributes and their capacity to convey meaning beyond their material substance. What do images show – and what are they about? In this way, the image functions similarly to the *sign*. The duality of the sign (see Figure 2) refers to the semiotic concept that a sign consists of two interconnected elements: the *signifier*, which is the form or expression (such as a word or image), and the *signified*, which is the meaning or concept that the sign represents as exemplified by the Swiss semiotician Ferdinand de Saussure to describe the relationship between images and language, essentially developing the concept of signs further (Davis & Hunt, 2017: 135).

The force of this duality in images has been succinctly expressed by Gottfried Boehm: 'Bilder sind spannungsgeladene, real-irreale Körper' (2007: 9), which is translated by us authors as 'images are bodies fraught with tension, simultaneously material and immaterial'. This duality underlines the complex nature of images, which can be both tangible or (as we may add) digital native objects and vehicles for abstract ideas. Alternatively, the physical image may be explained as a virtual stand-in for something lost and, thus, absent. Hans Belting takes the example of funereal images, where the missing body of the dead is replaced with an image of the dead: images, according to Belting, thus make a physical absence visible by transforming it into iconic presence (Belting, 2011: 3, 84ff.). As Boehm states, images are tension-filled entities, existing in a space where the material and immaterial, alternatively the real and the unreal, converge, challenging our perception but simultaneously cajoling deeper interpretation.

When thinking of images that comprise culture and are understood as art or heritage, their meaning can be complex, affected not only by their interpretation framework or their materiality but by the diversity of their significance across countries and contexts. More rigid definitions surrounding images as cultural heritage collections may in fact underscore their complex, multifarious interpretations. Cultural heritage for example is not a monolithic construct; our world is ever-changing and characterised by diversity in its expression. Artefacts, albeit visual expressions of identity and culture, often have complex provenance that makes them difficult to decode and to describe (Wagner et al., 2021: 604). Deciding assertively what an image entails, its interpretation is a complex endeavour for cultural heritage. Smith (2006: 28–30) discusses the concept of an Authorised Heritage Discourse (AHD). The AHD defines who the legitimate spokespersons for the past are and that affects how we unpack the qualities of images. Preserving art and heritage for future generations within this discourse limits its values and definitions to specific social groups and materiality. Smith argues that the practices of the AHD are linked to alienating a range of other social and cultural experiences such as the absence of gender, ethnicity, and class perspectives in heritage phenomena, as well as constraining and limiting their critique. The diversity that Smith highlights demonstrates a need for new ways of interpreting the past that consider cultural and social complexity. This is in line with the International Council of Museums' (ICOM) mandate on promoting diversity and inclusion as stated on the ICOM website. Mirroring this line of thought, Bia Mankell shows how theoretical, material, and practical perspectives intertwine in the visual arts and that these also have to do with other structures of sociocultural, economic, and political nature. To illustrate this, Mankell sees the image as a traversable place, a junction enabling communication where many actors move and where the image itself is an actor. As soon as the actors take possession of this open place, directional structures emerge, she states (Mankell, 2013: 9, 15). Such directional structures may appear very sudden for a beholder of an image. We would like to call this the *jack-in-the-box effect* of the image: as soon as you dare to open the box, you receive more than what you expected. During interpretation, the image develops into more tangled meanings, consciously or unconsciously.

Let us present one example of the drift or growth of meaning into a level of denser signification (see Figure 3).

When an image is understood by a person or a group of people, what structures can be analysed within the image? Building upon the notion of visual literacy, the nature of the structure is the next important question that naturally emerges. It is often assumed that structural complexity is inherent and hierarchical in visual representation. This hierarchical progression traverses from

MATERIALITY	SHOWN CONTENT (denotation)	IMPLIED CONTENT (connotation; context)
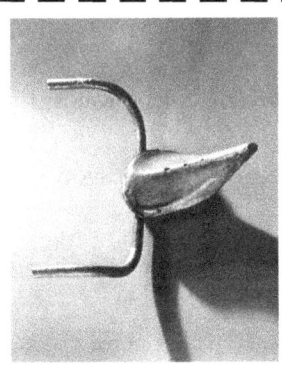 Handlebars and saddle Photography (black and white, 1940's style) Pixelated image with JPEG 'artefacts' on computer screen or alternatively, a printed rasterized CMYK image	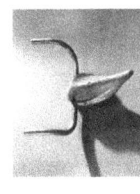 The object as a sculpture: Pablo Picasso, *Tête de taureau* (Bull's Head), assemblage, 1942, Musée Picasso, Paris  Any bull in real life: This specific bull is an 'Aurochs' bull at Parc animalier de Bouillon, Belgium	 The pictorial world of Modernist artist Pablo Picasso; all his images and self-representations of bulls and Minotaurs  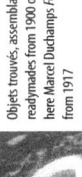 Objets trouvés, assemblages, and readymades from 1900 onwards; here Marcel Duchamps *Fountain* from 1917 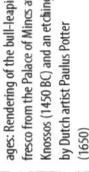  All depictions of bulls through the ages: Rendering of the bull-leaping fresco from the Palace of Minos at Knossos (1450 BC) and an etching by Dutch artist Paulus Potter (1650)   Bull horns as male attribute: 2021 Capitol rioter 'QAnon Shaman' (Jacob Chansley)

Figure 3 An example of image interpretation, from materiality to denotation, cultural implications, social and cultural context. The *objets trouvés* (lit. a natural or discarded objec: found by chance and held to have aesthetic value) of Picasso's handlebars and saddle resembles a bull, immediately alluding to contexts like male virility or Modernism. Illustration: J. v. Bonsdorff.

elemental forms and contrasts to established pictorial conventions, culminating in the potential revelation of extrinsic, or contextual, meaning. This hierarchical framework is similar to the model structure outlined by Erwin Panofsky or the condensed Panofsky/Shatford model. It is important to note that while Panofsky pays less attention to tangible materiality, his model provides a broad theory for deciphering meaning in fine art, while the Panofsky/Shatford version offers a specialised approach tailored to indexing and describing images in the domain of information retrieval (Panofsky, 1955; Shatford, 1986).

To return to AI, how does the complexity of our human interpretation of images map onto machines? An often-used concept in the field of computer vision is *ground truth*. Ground truth refers to the actual, real-world facts or accurate data used as a benchmark to train and evaluate machine learning models (Dumitrache et al., 2021; Krig, 2016: 247ff.). In the context of image processing or computer vision, ground truth data typically includes images that have been manually annotated or labelled to indicate the correct output for each input image. If one, for example, wants to detect cars in a satellite photo, one has to manually mark or label cars. These labels serve as the true answers the model needs to learn to predict. Of course, the real-world attachment to a degree applies to the study and classification of images as well. But historical development and user practices have turned images into diverse and differentiated tools of communication, like very different domains as, for example, calligraphy, baroque art, and Hallmark birthday cards, all with slowly evolving positions in a social matrix. Actually, something similar to ground truth could be found at different starting points in the graph on image meanings shown in Figure 3.

1. The physical reality and materiality of the object (the bicycle parts; side-stepping its capability of showing to something).
2. The object or topic the image signifies (the bull; leaving materiality as unimportant).
3. The set of pictorial conventions that are used to make the image readable and plausible.
4. The set of connotations or contextuality that pinpoint the image in a mental, social, or political matrix.

Thus, the interests of curators who are trained in the humanities are other than those of the ground truth concept used in computer vision studies. Instead of labelling 'truths', humans define a *focal point* for solving search or classification tasks when curating images within the art and cultural heritage sector. The primary focal point is determined by the interests and goals of the researcher or curator: it can be audience-driven, context-driven, or object-driven. There is no ground truth as such but only tasks relative to the expected outcome. Truths are therefore replaced by plausibility.

Building on the importance of images, but also emphasising the different possibilities that visual literacy for art and heritage may convey, instead of the concept of *ground truth* or any truth, we propose the notion of an *image framework*. Throughout this Element, an image framework refers to the theoretical and methodological scaffolding used to analyse and understand images across various dimensions, such as, for example, materiality, semantics, and functionality. It encompasses the intrinsic properties of the image, such as composition and colour, its extrinsic influences such as cultural and historical context, and the relationships between different modalities of representation. We use the concept of an image framework to help decode the layers of meaning embedded within images and how these meanings are packaged and disseminated to an audience. A multitude of frameworks, schemata, and models have been formulated in all disciplines dealing with images and visuality – especially within art history, psychology, semiotics, and media studies. Depending on the needs of, for example, the curator, researcher, or pedagogue, different frameworks may be considered. In the selection of image frameworks it is essential to evaluate which content is most conducive for managing and describing visual objects – in the current case – within the context of a cultural heritage institution. Beyond the obvious metadata, that is image descriptions, or clusters of descriptions such as provenance, dates, even material properties, the discussion extends to the significance of various structural levels all of which hold possible relevance for machine learning applications. However, the focus initially centres on the visible pictorial conventions readily discernible from the image itself, followed by an exploration of the extrinsic factors influencing image appreciation, such as the requisite circumstantial knowledge.

At this juncture, the highlighted levels of pictorial conventions and circumstantial knowledge offer the richest trove of pertinent information and meaningful descriptions necessary for machine learning within a cultural heritage framework. Hans Belting's anthropological notion of the image can be mentioned again in this connection. For Belting humans do not only possess but actively generate images and sensory perceptions through cognitive processes, effectively employing the brain as a living medium (Belting, 2005). Further, Belting's approach to images underscores the idea that humans inherently create and rely on images not merely as artistic expressions but as fundamental components of cognition and communication. This view brings to the forefront the critical role images play in constructing our perception of reality and shaping our world views. By taking this concept to heart, one embraces the belief that images can encapsulate complex ideas, such as religions, cultural narratives, philosophy, and so on, which are crucial to understanding human culture and thought. Embedded within this perspective is a fundamental principle of this Element, *to take the world view of images seriously*. This guiding motif permeates our discourse, encouraging an appreciation for the potential deeper layers of meaning embedded within visual representations.

Firstly, there is no general rule, no quick fixes, for how images can be handled with AI tools: approaching images deserve different mindsets, different image frameworks, depending on the complexity of content and the goals of the curator. Secondly, it must be emphasised that taking images seriously means that one should respect the *possibility* of images being complex and to carry deeper meaning. An initial respect for images means that one is equipped for unexpected interpretive richness. This viewpoint underscores the significance of acknowledging the epistemological functions of images as well as their role in shaping social perspectives – thus, packaging and condensing the human condition in visual form. Thirdly, an image is not the same as the mentioned image framework which we see as a frame of mind in dealing with the image. Before formulating what may constitute adequate descriptions of visual cultural heritage objects, we have to make clear that when assessing the properties of an image, we ought to remember that an image framework implies different things for different stakeholders. An image framework can take different forms across different disciplines, for example, media history, semiotics, archiving, museology, and information technology.

Speaking of scholarship, art history, media studies, semiotics, archiving, museology, and IT science use different frameworks. Sometimes models are preconceived without closer explanations. Here for brevity's sake, we leave out anthropology, cognitive psychology, psychoanalysis, neurobiology, neuropsychology, linguistics, and philosophy. But even focusing on the target audience of this book, art historians, semioticians, archivists, museologists, other heritage professionals and computer scientists expect different results from studying the image and thus have different perceptions. As it may be observed in Tables 1a–1 c, some scholars base their assumptions on psychological foundations (Arnheim and Gombrich). Other scholars conceptualise the image as a text: then we have to ask ourselves what place context does take in the image framework. Otherwise expressed, what are the connections between the intrinsic and extrinsic, sometimes expressed as denotative and connotative features? Although these concepts have distinct scopes, they overlap in terms of how they contribute to understanding and interpreting images. While intrinsic/denotative features emphasise observable elements, extrinsic/connotative features delve into contextual or symbolic meanings (Panofsky and Shatford). Denotative features are the explicit, literal, and readily observable aspects of the

Table 1a The chart exemplifies a selection of image frameworks used by early twentieth-century art historians

Scholar	Image Framework	Key Concepts
Erwin Panofsky	Iconography/ Iconology	Panofsky's method examines three levels of image interpretation: primary or natural subject matter, iconography (subject, symbolism), and iconology (cultural context, deep meanings).
Rudolf Arnheim	Gestalt and Visual Perception	Arnheim's theory emphasises Gestalt psychology, focusing on how visual elements like shape, form, and structure create meaning. His approach looks at perceptual organisation in images.
E. H. Gombrich	Art and Perception	Gombrich's work explores how people perceive art, emphasising the role of context and culture in shaping perception. He examined the history of art with an emphasis on narrative, cultural context, and artistic development.

image – like objects, people, or scenes – echoing the phenomenal world in Plato's philosophy mentioned above. In the same way, connotative features point to the deeper symbolic and contextual meanings of an image, akin to the noumenal, where the true essence or form lies. Connotations might require interpretation, relying on knowledge beyond the immediate visuals, just as the noumenal requires philosophical insight to grasp its essence.

The selection of frameworks in the tables above is in no way exhaustive. Our point is that they are to a certain point interchangeable due to the needs of the researcher or curator. As stated above, there are no universal guidelines or quick solutions for managing images with AI tools: different approaches and frameworks are required, varying with the content's materiality, descriptive complexity, and the curator's or researcher's objectives and motives. Furthermore, the examples of image frameworks we show above may *all* be used in a context of machine learning. The usefulness of any given pre-conceived image framework must be determined by the immediate needs of stakeholders, such as the goal of the task or possible audiences (cf. concluding chapter). We ask ourselves: What interest do the stakeholders take in their visual sources? Is it how the images

Table 1b The chart exemplifies a selection of image frameworks used by mid twentieth-century scholars.

Sara Shatford/ Erwin Panofsky	Faceted Approach for Information Retrieval	This model, developed by Sara Shatford with influence from Panofsky, categorises image description into four facets: who, what, where, and when. It allows for systematic indexing and retrieval.
Susan Sontag	Photography and Social Critique	Sontag's approach examines the social and ethical implications of photography, focusing on how images can shape public perception, influence memory, and carry political or ideological messages. She explores the impact of photography on society and its capacity to manipulate or evoke emotions.
Roland Barthes	Semiotics and Mythology	Barthes analysed the construction of meaning through signs and explored the concept of 'myth' in visual media. His work focuses on the connotative and denotative levels of meaning in images, emphasising the role of cultural context and the social construction of reality.

physically appear, what they show, what they are about, or how this information is structured or communicated?

Let us break this down for different domains: *art historians* tend to see images as carriers of historically changing pictorial conventions, formalism, and historical and cultural significance. The art historian Belting comments that traditional art theory would have strong reservations about any image theory that threatens the old monopoly of art and its exclusive subject matter (2005). This kind of territorial thinking may not be maintained in the light of alternative media, besides visual arts, since the nineteenth century at least. *Media historians* often stress the media *per se* and the technical side of image transmission. *Semioticians* approach images as systems of signs. They are interested in how meaning is constructed through structural concepts present in the image, like the semiotic distinctions between the syntactic (structural), semantic (meaning-related), and pragmatic (use and effect) dimensions of an image. But, according to Hans Belting, they do not allow images to exist beyond 'the controllable territory of signs, signals, and communication' (2005). *Poststructuralists* in different academic disciplines use semiotic terms to a certain degree but concentrate on larger questions like discourses of power and other master signifiers, often side-stepping

Table 1c The chart exemplifies a selection of image frameworks used by late twentieth century to early twenty-first century scholars

Umberto Eco	Semiotics and Interpretation	Eco's semiotic model views images as systems of signs. He explores the ambiguity of images and the process of interpretation, emphasising the role of the observer in creating meaning.
W. J. T. Mitchell	Pictorial Turn and Visual Culture	Mitchell focuses on the 'pictorial turn', exploring the role of images in shaping cultural narratives. His work investigates how images create, reflect, and challenge ideologies and discourses.
Judith Butler	Gender and Visual Representation	Butler's work delves into the ways images construct and reinforce gender identities. Her approach involves analysing visual culture through the lens of gender theory, exploring how images perpetuate or challenge traditional gender norms. She emphasises the performative aspects of gender and its representation in images and media.
Hans Belting	Anthropology of Images	Belting's model explores the role of images in human culture from an anthropological perspective. He examines the fundamental relation of image, body, and medium in every attempt of picture-making.

features inherent in the media proper. *Archivists and heritage curators* may view images in terms of their classification, authenticity, domains, and provenance. *Museologists* may focus on the preservation, display and interpretation of images for public engagement. Last, *computer scientists* are often more concerned with the technical aspects of handling the image than any image theory or image frameworks: digitisation, storage, metadata, structured and machine readable information and retrieval take precedence, even if computer vision and human computer interaction are research fields in their own right.

In a perfect future world, image interpretations can be fluid and interdisciplinary rather than rigid. For example, art historians and semioticians could develop a stronger interest in the materiality of the object, and computer scientists could be more informed on pictorial conventions and cultural connotations. Art historians may be aware of the dichotomy between the physical meaning-carrier and the meaning itself. In turn, computer scientists do take the question of the *semantic gap* earnestly in consideration: The semantic gap implies the discrepancy between the information that can be derived from low-level image data (colour, shapes) and the interpretation that human viewers of an image base on their visual literacy and cultural competence. Again, speaking in the domain of cultural heritage, we need to stress that the image framework should encompass the aspect of tangible materiality (see Figure 3). The image framework should also acknowledge the convergence of various visual cultures, where the focus shifts from, e. g., the style or historical context of objects to, more importantly, how individuals and communities integrate these visual elements into their personal or shared spheres of identity (Johannesson, 1991: 11).

As this Element and our analysis progresses, we argue and advocate that for aforementioned reasons AI requires both diverse and specific input from the humanities: The pre-conceived image frameworks mentioned above should play a more important role when developing image analysis algorithms. The researcher's or curator's attitude to the image is relative depending on the complexity of the image and the actual situation of the image's presentation and interpretation as well as other external circumstances such as prevailing internal scientific, political, and ideological discourses: hence, the need of interchangeable image frameworks explained above. But before moving on to discussing the possibilities that arise with computer vision, it is important to state the fact that an image provides humans with information which is packaged in ways that make it understood by different people and groups. Here, we would like to point out the brevity of meanings and interpretations we mentioned earlier: images – or rather, their interpretations – can start from a latent quality, a mere potential, and quite suddenly emerge as full-blown, qualified meaning-carriers. Indeed, if the image is packaged in an effective way, the beholder always gets more than asked for – this is the surprise effect of the *jack-in-the-box* quality of the image (Oestreicher & von Bonsdorff, 2022).

In what follows, we become more concrete: we move into a description of how computer vision may work and how it may be understood by generalists if pitted against human vision. Providing classification as an example, we return to art and heritage images and image datasets to illustrate the complexities that arise when we develop systems that aim to identify, to describe, interpret, and to classify images.

2 Current Trends on AI and Art and Culture

2.1 AI and Visual Heritage: An Overview

2.1.1 Charting the Uses: AI, Art, and Visual Heritage

In the first section we introduced a number of concepts. First, we described the importance of visual literacy and coined image frameworks to show the variety of scholarly interpretation and at the same time the complexity of meanings that an image may elicit. We now delve deeper into how computers 'see'. In other words, we discuss how computer vision works and how it may be understood by generalists if pitted against human vision. In doing so, we move forward to discuss the legacy and trends in applications of AI methods and tools with some notable examples of implementation in the arts and the cultural heritage sector. The ambition of the authors is that such trends will not be merely seen as contemporary implementations that are solely representative of the time of writing this Element but hopefully will further provide readers with an insight on technological development for the next few decades. To think of images within art and heritage datasets in the context of recent technological development, especially AI, is a timely and worthy enterprise.

In the time of writing this Element, heritage organisations continue to undergo rapid digital transformation. Collections are continuously and increasingly digitised, and this affects how collections are managed, curated and communicated with the public (Foka, Attemark, & Wahlberg, 2022: 66–85; Foka et al., 2023; Murphy & Villaespesa, 2020; Tzouganatou, 2018: 377–383, 2021). In the future we envisage AI to be used increasingly in the art and heritage sector due to an expansion in digitisation and the conversion of collections to data but also the increasingly large amount of born-digital image datasets. By born-digital, we refer to those images that are created and distributed in a digital format. The aim of AI implementation in the cultural and creative sectors more generally is preoccupied with the concepts of autonomy and adaptivity, automating tasks that would otherwise require enormous amounts of work to be completed, for example, the classification of large datasets, the transcription of archives that are handwritten, or the accurate restoration of frescoes that are partially destroyed by environmental change. We hereby stress that as image collections vary greatly so does the implementation of tools and methods. In turn, formats but also concepts of reasoning, classification, knowledge representation, curation, or learning may also be different. In practice, recent implementation and related research shows a lot of potential. In what follows we look at how AI technologies are currently implemented for image datasets in the art and heritage sector focusing on the

Table 2 Charting the Uses of AI and Heritage, The author's own charting of AI implementation for the heritage sector, based on the *Commission study on Opportunities, and challenges of artificial intelligence technologies for the cultural and creative sectors*, 2022. Accessible at https://www.europarl.europa.eu/thinktank/en/document/EPRS_BRI(2023)747120

Curation and Conservation (Archival, Cataloguing, Information Management)	Visitor Experience Management	Audience Engagement Activities
Computer vision for identifying, cataloguing, and enriching collections with additional information (metadata)	Tracking visitor numbers	Reimagine, reinterpret the collection
Natural Language Processing (NLP) to interpret text based work, e.g. Recognition/Translation/Transcription	Forecasting attendance	Personalise visitor experience
Image Analysis	Analysing feedback from visitors (sentiment analysis)	
Examination, Conservation & Restoration		
Object detection		

guidelines and descriptions provided already by researchers and are in line with how the European Commission surveys these technologies.

According to the European Commission study of opportunities, AI implementation is divided into three categories (see Table 2): the first one is curation and conservation, sometimes referred to as archival, cataloguing, and information management. This, dependent on the dataset in question, may include computer vision and image analysis methods for the examination, conservation and restoration of images. The second one concerns visitor experience management such as, for example, tracking visitor numbers. The final way of implementing AI concerns audience engagement activities such as reimagining and interpreting the collection or personalising visitor experience.

Studies on the use of AI in the transcription and translation of ancient texts and inscriptions that utilise image analysis, otherwise known as Handwritten Text Recognition, are many (Assael et al., 2022: 280–283; Chammas et al., 2022: 30769–30784; Fu, 2022: 11, 45; Guidi et al., 2023: 16, 79; León et al., 2023: 788–795; Locaputo, 2023: 68–76; Marchant, 2023; Roueché, 2022: 235–236; Sanders et al., 2018: 1–5; Shaus et al., 2020: 15). Research on the application of AI in the classification and reconstruction of pottery and other artefacts presents an interesting and ever-evolving field where specific datasets, if large and well structured, may help train specific tasks (Anglisano, 2022; Aoulalay et al., 2020: 1–7; Argyrou et al., 2023; Bickler, 2018: 20–32; Cardarelli, 2022; Chetouani et al., 2020: 1–7; Cintas, 2020: 106–112; Kuntitan et al., 2022: 1–15; Marie et al., 2005: 1527–1533; Ostertag et al., 2020: 336–340). The central technology that is used for these aforementioned applications, deciphering ancient text, and for identification, classification, and even reconstruction of artefacts is computer vision.

2.1.2 Image Meets Computer Vision: Classification as Example

Classification is the process of identifying and grouping entities, for example, objects or ideas into predetermined categories based on their key characteristics. But scientific classification and taxonomies of sorts differ over time and across disciplines. Classification is casually or formally based on agreed-upon categories among disciplines and their respective scientific communities which may change over time. For example, Linnaeus' classification schemes for living organisms and animals replaced older Aristotelian models. Classification schemes for heritage collections can vary based on different aspects. One common classification scheme used in the context of pictorial heritage collections is a decimal classification scheme, similar to the Dewey Decimal classification scheme used in libraries. In this scheme, single digits or pairs of digits represent broad subject areas, with longer numbers starting with those digits representing subsets of that subject area. This classification system emphasises the subjects depicted in the images, particularly in the context of pictorial collections like the FSA-OWI – The Farm Security Administration – Office of War Information Photograph Collection (https://www.loc.gov/collections/fsa-owi-black-and-white-negatives/about-this-collection). This collection offers a comprehensive visual documentation of American life from 1935 to 1944.

Major subject classes in this scheme include categories such as The Land, Cities and Towns, People, Homes and Living Conditions, Transportation, Work, Organized Society, War, Medicine and Health, Intellectual and Creative Activity, Social and Personal Activity, and an Alphabetical Section for subjects not covered adequately by the main classes. Each major subject class is further subdivided into smaller subclasses to provide more detailed categorization within each subject area.

Using a standard classification scheme in heritage institutions offers several benefits, enhancing various aspects of museum operations and collections management. Firstly, a classification system provides a hierarchical arrangement of records, making it easier to work with record groups and facilitating curatorial study, research, evaluation, assessment of collections, exhibition development, and media and visitor engagement. Think of a tabular dataset – essentially an excel file – where everything is organised by distinct categories. Secondly, such systems enable museums to categorise objects based on their functional context, allowing for a more organised and structured approach to managing collections. This structured classification helps in providing a general overview of the entire collection and facilitates access by allowing users to search for objects of the same type or kind that are related to each other. Moreover, standard classification schemes like the *Nomenclature for Museum Cataloging* are essential for ensuring consistency and precision in naming objects within collections, aiding in the identification and cataloguing of human-made objects in a systematic manner (Dunn & Bouchier, 2020). These systems also streamline the exchange of collection data among museums or departments, enhancing collaboration and information sharing within the museum community. Additionally, the use of a standard classification scheme helps museums maintain internal consistency in object classification and naming, ensuring that the chosen system is consistently applied to the museum's collection, thus improving overall collection management and accessibility. The benefits of using a standard classification scheme in museums include improved organisation and accessibility of collections, enhanced curatorial study and research, streamlined data exchange among institutions, and increased consistency and precision in object naming and cataloguing processes.

Overall, humans classify to describe and to catalogue based on experience and expertise and with the purpose to organise knowledge for themselves and others. A prime example of a comprehensive standard classification system for images is, at the time of writing, ICONCLASS (https://iconclass.org/), which provides subject access to the collections of many museums and libraries. It was developed starting in the 1940s by Henri van de Waal, a professor of art history at Leiden University, and is maintained by the Henri van de Waal Foundation. ICONCLASS consists of an alphanumeric class number, or notation, and a corresponding content definition, a textual correlate, to describe the subject matter of visual works. ICONCLASS covers a broad spectrum of visual communication, beyond just the traditional cultural heritage domain. It has over 28,000 specific categories organised in a hierarchical structure. ICONCLASS works by breaking down complex visual subjects into a hierarchical tree structure of meanings, allowing for detailed cataloguing. One example of this branching and subdivisions would be 'Society, Civilization, Culture – Family, Descendance – Betrothal and Marriage – Wedding Feast'. Many museums and libraries, such as the Rijksmuseum, Städel Museum, and Herzog Anton Ulrich-Museum, use ICONCLASS to index and provide access to their art collections. It is further important to note that the most recent ICONCLASS PLUS edition includes further machine vision features, which at the time of writing are available to paying customers.

So humans and institutions describe and classify image datasets. But what about machines? Can machines describe and classify with the same brevity as humans? If so, how does machine or computer vision work? Research has shown that the classification or identification of images is based upon 'the development or implementation of feature extraction/learning based on one type of feature or, more commonly, a combination of features' (Wasielewski, 2023a: 4). By features, developers tend to mean characteristics of a visual image that make it distinct from another image. These may include but are not limited to colour, grayscale gradients, edges, texture and scale, and luminance. These features could be numerical and understood via pixels or represented as a kind of chart called a histogram. Different features that are used for image identification or classification can be 'global and include the entire image or local and be concerned with only a part of it' (Wasielewski, 2023a: 4–5). Classification for images that is done computationally, specifically image classification, is the process of assigning a label or class to an entire image based on its content. This task involves categorising and labelling groups of pixels or vectors within an image according to specific rules, enabling the identification of what is depicted in the image. Image classification models analyse the content of an image and predict which class or label the image belongs to, providing valuable insights and enabling various applications in computer vision and artificial intelligence. To return to the materiality to context scheme we presented earlier, typically such features are mostly low level and can be mapped as denotative practice.

Image classification should be distinguished computationally from object detection and object localization. These are fundamental concepts in computer vision and image annotation, each serving distinct purposes in analysing visual data. Image classification involves assigning a single label to an entire image based on its content. This task aims to categorise images into predefined classes or categories, such as identifying whether an image contains a cat or a dog. It focuses on recognizing the overall content of the image without specifying the location of individual objects within it. Object detection, on the other hand, goes a step further than image classification by not only identifying the objects present in an image but also locating them within the image. This task involves detecting multiple objects of interest and drawing bounding boxes around them to precisely outline their positions. Object detection is crucial for scenarios where multiple objects need to be identified and located within an image. Object localization is a more specific task within object detection that focuses on accurately pinpointing the location of a particular object or region of interest within an image. It involves not only detecting the presence of objects but also providing detailed spatial information by drawing precise bounding boxes around them. Object localisation enables more granular analysis and understanding of the spatial layout of objects within an image. By understanding the distinctions between image classification, object detection, and object localisation, one can effectively leverage these concepts in various applications of computer vision, from basic image categorisation to detailed object localization for tasks like autonomous driving, medical imaging, and surveillance systems.

Classification, in turn, may simplify tasks by categorising data into two classes. It is commonly used for problems requiring yes/no answers. Again, there are different ways in which classification operates that concerns the type of classification. Multiclass classification extends beyond binary by categorising data into three or more classes. It finds applications in fields like NLP for example, recognising words in a historical archive via sentiment analysis to classify, for example, work tasks described into various categories of occupations. In multilabel classification, items can have multiple labels, unlike multiclass, where each item belongs to a single class. For instance, classifying image colours where an image can have multiple colours like red, orange, yellow, and purple simultaneously. Finally, hierarchical classification organises classes into a hierarchy based on similarities. Higher-level classes represent broader categories, while lower-level classes are more specific. This structure is akin to organising fruits where higher levels may be fruits in general and lower levels could be specific types like apples or oranges.

For classification success, however, if it may be defined as such, one needs to ensure that descriptive data on those images are of high quality. Quality is crucial for classification tasks, significantly impacting the performance of classifiers. High-quality data enhances classification accuracy and efficiency by enabling models to make more accurate predictions. Research indicates that the choice of a classifier becomes less critical when good feature selection methods are applied before classification, especially on high-dimensional datasets. Additionally, improving data quality through processes like feature selection can lead to similar results across different classifiers, highlighting the importance of working with higher-quality data (Morán-Fernández et al., 2022: 365–375). Data quality is emphasised in machine learning projects, with poor-quality data negatively affecting model performance, reliability, and scalability. In computer vision projects, data quality is essential for success, influencing model performance, reliability, and ethical considerations. Therefore, making sure cultural heritage datasets are coherently and carefully curated and annotated at all stages of a project by subject experts, from acquisition to deployment, is vital for achieving accurate and reliable classification results.

But what happens when classification schemes are applied to art and heritage datasets? The essential question 'Can machines automatically classify artefacts?' should be answered with a 'yes', but include a reservation. Computer vision can classify historical datasets with accuracy, provided the data is of high quality and already wealthy in descriptions by subject experts. By employing deep learning methods, computer vision models can effectively analyse and recognize historical documents, enabling tasks like character recognition, style classification, manuscript dating, semantic segmentation, and content-based retrieval. However, one challenge is the need for a large amount of training data to achieve satisfactory performance in both face recognition and object detection systems. Another challenge is the choice between classic, non-learned approaches and other machine learning algorithms – where deep learning is a sophisticated subset of machine learning that utilises multi-layered neural networks to simulate the complex decision-making capabilities of the human brain which we develop more in Section 2.2. While deep learning algorithms tend to outperform other machine learning in terms of accuracy and development time, they have higher resource requirements and are limited to performing within their training space. Additional issue is that heritage and art historical collections are so idiosyncratic in nature that what works for one dataset may not be working for another (see Foka et al., 2023).

But can machines automatically classify cultural heritage datasets based on specific classification standards? In theory, this could be achieved, provided there are large training datasets that are richly and consistently annotated in ways that fit those standards and further by making such datasets and their metadata machine readable. For example, let us return to ICONCLASS. While ICONCLASS has been used successfully for higher-level categories, automatically classifying works into its more specific subcategories has proven challenging due to the complex hierarchical structure but also the material and epistemological complexity of artefacts. Furthermore, in ICONCLASS each image or image concept is provided additionally with a unique reference to subject heading Uniform Resource Identifier (URI). It is also possible to retrieve machine-readable formats, by appending either .rdf or .json to the URI that can then be picked by other systems, for example, Europeana, or Google Arts and Culture. It is, however, also possible that in aggregators as such or recommender systems, bias in these classification standards may be augmented, as we will discuss further in Section 3.

Computer vision has emerged as a powerful tool for classifying and enriching online collections by automatically generating descriptions or tags to make images more discoverable.

But can machines, computers, be entirely autonomous in terms of image classification? One major historical impetus for the development of AI is the wish for self-regulating or feedback systems – that are to a great extent autonomous. The technical evolution of the concept of feedback can be traced through separate ancestral lines, such as the water clock, the thermostat, and mechanisms for controlling windmills (Mayr, 1970). A related sub-set of the feedback system is the notion of breathing life into a non-living counterpart: think of Ovid's Pygmalion, the sculptor who falls in love with his statue, which is then brought to life. The modern-day living counterpart is the robot (Bredekamp, 2010). Both the longing for a living counterpart and a wish for autonomous, responsible systems may have a bearing on our discussion on what to expect and what not to expect from AI-based systems intended for use within the cultural heritage sector. At this point, we will not endorse fully autonomous systems. We would rather stress the aspect of the AI tools and their capacity to assist humans in their tasks. Therefore we fully support human supervision and discernment at every stage in the use of AI tools. We find that systems should be meticulously curated and fine-honed so as to enable automatic, but still supervised, classifications and searches on visual cultural heritage materials.

So what is possible for the moment using computer vision within the cultural heritage sector? Instead of a detailed assessment, we have chosen to illustrate possibilities within the field with a rough graphical estimate (see Figure 4). Museums and institutions interested in leveraging AI technologies may use it

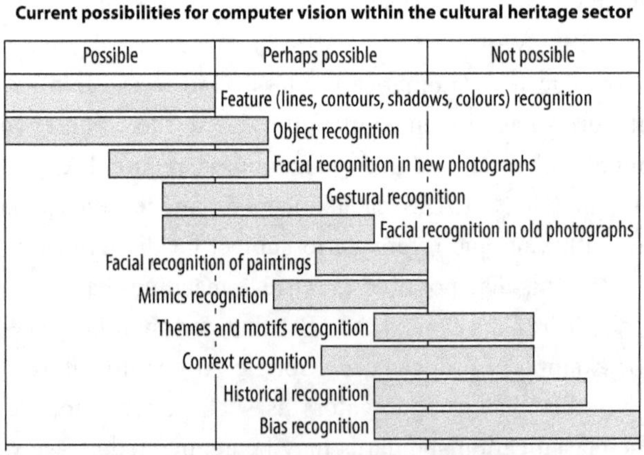

Figure 4 Possibilities of using AI and computer vision as for now (2024). Illustration: J. v. Bonsdorff.

with caution, since the field is in rapid development. From the left column, 'what is possible', the areas of interest become more complex and difficult for computer vision, landing in the right column, 'what is currently not possible'. At the same time, the graphic highlights areas where AI is already making significant contributions and those where human input remains indispensable. Roughly, we follow the scheme from shown content to implied content as in Figure 3.

We have chosen some examples on handling images depicting humans from different ages: facial recognition in modern photographs (from 1950 onwards) is highly accurate due to the higher quality of images and the sheer abundance of photos in recent decades. On the other hand, gestural recognition, while possible, presents greater challenges due to the dynamic nature of human gestures. This would require AI systems to perform temporal data analysis (read: film or comics) to accurately interpret motion and gestures, which is more complex than static image recognition. Recognising faces in older photographs, particularly those taken between 1840 and 1950, poses additional difficulties due to lower image quality and variations in photographic techniques. However, AI can still perform facial recognition on these images with reasonable accuracy, provided the models are trained on datasets that point out historical variances. Facial recognition in paintings would be more challenging still, given the artistic styles, abstractions, and pictorial conventions from different ages that differ significantly from current depictions. While AI can identify patterns and similarities, it struggles with abstract or heavily stylised representations. Here, as always, the rule applies that the better the datasets are curated and annotated when preparing for machine learning, the better the results are.

Mimics recognition, which involves interpreting facial expressions and emotions, is another complex task due to the subtle variations in expressions across different individuals and cultural contexts. Although AI can identify basic emotions, it often struggles with nuanced expressions, especially in premodern art. Iconographical recognition, which deals with identifying themes, motifs, or topoi, requires understanding symbolic and thematic elements used in art and cultural artefacts. This is difficult for AI to achieve without extensive contextual knowledge and specific training on iconography datasets.

Context recognition entails understanding the broader setting and implications of an image, a task that requires AI to integrate multimodal data. Although AI is beginning to explore this area, comprehensive context interpretation remains a challenging frontier (cf. Section 3.2.1). Historical recognition demands a deep understanding of historical knowledge and interpretation, capabilities that current AI models are not yet fully equipped to handle without human input.

Finally, bias recognition from a current viewpoint (in our case, 2024) is a complex undertaking that involves identifying and analysing biases present in images. This task requires an understanding of societal and cultural nuances, which AI can partially assist with, but ultimately necessitates human oversight and contextual awareness to interpret and address effectively. It is clear to us that the areas to the right of the graphic are those that primarily should be the aim of new development for AI tools in the cultural heritage sector.

To conclude, if computer vision is properly implemented, it may help raise central concerns for heritage collections, particularly those containing images. However, a technological paradigm based on the assumption that an image can be classified in unambiguous terms by machine-generated keywords will have persistent challenges when applied to visual art, which is characterised by resisting simple and stable interpretations. To apply computer vision intended for image recognition in a meaningful way that furthers interpretation, technology must be developed to incorporate complex and non-binary, non-stereotypical interpretations. In this vein, concepts such as postcolonial sociotechnical (STS) theories, postcolonial computing, and decolonial computing are approaches centred on 'using technologies for undoing the technologies of colonialism' (Risam, 2018: 79–81). To summarise: in this section we discussed, among other things, how computer vision works in terms of classification and object detection – and that given the complexity of art and cultural datasets, autonomy might not be something that could be easily implemented at present. In what follows, we discuss some success stories to counterbalance the limitations posed with potential.

2.1.3 AI and Image and Heritage: Success Stories

At the time of writing this Element several museums are experimenting with such AI approaches to enhance their digital collections. The National Gallery of Denmark has used off-the-shelf computer vision software to categorise every single work in their online collection, which contains approximately 40,000 digitised works. This has enabled online visitors to search for works in new ways, such as by motifs, colour schemes, or visual similarity (https://www.smk.dk/en/article/artificial-intelligence-helps-organise-denmarks-largest-art-collection/). Harvard Art Museums use computer vision to categorise artwork and make their collections more widely accessible. Well-known museums, including the Metropolitan Museum of Art, the Museum of Modern Art in New York, and the Rijksmuseum in Amsterdam, have also used computer vision methods to make datasets available for research, including through competitions.

A large AI may further help with restoration, reconstruction and preservation as well as prediction of damage. Sensor data and AI algorithms can be used to perform predictive modelling, that is, to model how artefacts age and deteriorate over time. This allows conservators to predict future damage and to take preventative measures, or to determine the best treatments to minimise existing damage while preserving the current appearance. Curators further leverage image analysis tools to examine and to study visual artefacts in greater detail, extracting valuable insights and information from artworks, photographs, and other visual materials. Conservators and curators may use AI to restore artefacts as well as to predict their future in times of climate transition and environmental change (Mishra, 2021: 227–245.). AI has been used in several ways to help restore and preserve art and cultural heritage artefacts. AI algorithms can analyse photos of damaged paintings and use machine learning to fill in missing or damaged areas, digitally reconstructing what the original would have looked like (Gaber et al., 2023: 185–190).

For archaeological artefacts that contain images like pottery or mosaics that have been broken into many fragments, AI can help solve the puzzle by analysing the shapes and patterns to determine how the pieces fit together. Projects like RePAIR and Scan4Reco use AI, robotics, and 3D scanning to virtually reassemble artefacts (Poulopoulos, 2022: 73). Laser scanning, photogrammetry, and other digital techniques are being used to create high-resolution 3D models and digital archives of cultural heritage sites and artefacts. This helps preserve a record of the objects and enables further study and virtual exhibition. Examples include digitising the Mogao Caves in China and the Rijksmuseum's restoration of Rembrandt's *The Night Watch* (Van den Heuvel et al., 2021: 99–141). Deep Neural Networks (DNNs) have been used to recognize pottery types and decorations (Gualandi et al., 2021; Zhao et al., 2024). Virtual reconstruction based on generative adversarial networks has been applied to pottery (Navarro et al., 2022) and coins (Zachariou, 2020). AI has also enhanced the collection of ceramic data (van Helden, 2022). Supervised learning approaches, including machine and deep learning, have been explored for point cloud semantic segmentation of 3D architectural components (Pierdicca et al., 2020). Convolutional Neural Networks (CNNs) have been employed for various archaeological detection tasks. Aerial laser scanning (ALS, LiDAR) data has been utilised to detect barrows and Celtic fields in the Netherlands (Verschoof-van der Vaart & Lambers, 2019). CNNs have also been applied for the semantic segmentation of Ground Penetrating Radar (GPR) anomalies on archaeological sites, both on radargrams (B-scans) and more recently on 2D time/depth slices (C-scans) (Küçükdemirci & Sarris, 2022). Notably an overview of how AI is used in the intersection of archaeology and cultural heritage in terms of computer vision applications may be found in Landeschi (2023: 197–216).

A notable example of machine learning applied for images for educational purposes in the field of cultural heritage concerns ARsinoë— an application that uses machine learning and image detection for learning Egyptian Hieroglyphs with Augmented Reality and Machine Learning (Plecher et al., 2020: 326–332). The Arsinoë application utilises machine learning and image detection to enhance its functionality. It begins with data collection, gathering a large dataset of relevant images – in this case hieroglyphs. These images are used to train machine learning models through supervised learning, where the model learns to recognize patterns and features by analysing labelled images. The trained model then extracts key features from new images for accurate detection and classification. The image detection process involves pre-processing images to improve quality and consistency, using techniques like resizing and noise reduction. Advanced detection algorithms, such as convolutional neural networks (CNNs), scan the images for specific patterns and features. Once detected, the application classifies the images based on these patterns. The workflow includes users uploading images, the application processing them with the trained model and detection algorithms, and then providing results such as identified objects and classifications. This integration of machine learning and image detection improves accuracy, efficiency, and scalability, making the Arsinoë application suitable for various uses in the cultural heritage sector more generally.

A larger initiative is the European Time Machine project (https://www.time machine.eu/unleashing-big-data-of-the-past-europe-builds-a-time-machine/). The European Commission has selected Time Machine as one of six key proposals to shape large-scale research initiatives over the coming decade. This initiative, which has been allocated 1 million euro for the development of comprehensive roadmaps, aims to harness and leverage the Big Data of history. Time Machine is set to pioneer new digitisation and AI technologies to unlock the treasures within Europe's extensive cultural heritage, ensuring open and equitable access to information that will bolster future scientific and technological progress in Europe. Work within the Time Machine framework shows how AI is a powerful tool, but it requires expert input from researchers to succeed, thus advocating for how the human factor remains essential in the development and application of AI technologies.

Another successful implementation is the detection of hidden archaeological sites. In the Utrechtse Heuvelrug and Veluwe areas of the Netherlands, forests have helped preserve archaeological artefacts from human activities, but also made them difficult to discover. The LiDAR (Light Detection and Ranging) method, which enables research in locations where archaeological remains are concealed by vegetation, has been used to create high-resolution elevation maps. Researchers at Leiden University's Leiden Centre of Data Science (LCDS) and the Data Science Research Programme (DSRP) at the Faculty of Archaeology developed a flexible, robust, and automatic detection method for archaeological objects using both LiDAR data and R-CNN (region-based convolutional neural network) techniques (see Verschoof-Van der Vaart, 2019).

The iART (https://www.iart.vision/) project has created an e-research tool designed to enhance the use and analysis of image data within humanities research. The goal of iART is to refine the exploration of electronic image databases, elevating the efficiency of current scientific information systems (Springstein et al., 2021). The open Web platform implemented the CLIP algorithm early in 2021: iArt performs differentiated fine art searches, using a complex modular system architecture. The iArt search engine masters iconographically based classification principles that, for example, examine objects for biblical motifs, general genre themes, and free-form prompts as well as combinations with image searches – but essentially utilising AI generative technology. Last, but certainly not least, AI chatbots and augmented reality are being used in museums to provide interactive storytelling concerning images and to answer visitor questions about the artworks. For example, the Pinacoteca de São Paulo Museum in Brazil saw a 200% per cent increase in visitors after deploying an AI-powered audio guide called The Voice of Art (Perra, 2022: 685–693)

We hope to have provided a few examples of success stories, yet we need to stress that one must always bear in mind that when it comes to computer vision, one key complexity arises from the nature of the images themselves. While image recognition algorithms have achieved impressive performance in classifying and detecting objects in photographic images, they still struggle to recognise objects in non-photographic depiction styles, such as paintings and drawings. This is sometimes referred to as 'the cross-depiction problem', and it remains a significant obstacle to the use of image recognition in art collections. An interesting attempt to address this challenge has been presented by Brighton Museum (UK), which has experimented with using off-the-shelf software to offer suggestions for metadata as a provocation to inspire human curators to include keywords they otherwise might not have thought of (Foka et al., 2023: 815–825). Additionally, if images involve text, NLP techniques are further employed to interpret, to translate, and to transcribe text-based works in museum collections, such as manuscripts, historical documents, and literary pieces, enhancing accessibility and understanding. In what follows, we provide a simplified and comprehensive overview of how these technologies work so as to ease into Section 3 which concerns both pitfalls and potentials of AI technologies for art and heritage.

2.2 Technologies and Methods for Computer Vision

Leaving AI implementation aside for the moment, we turn to more technical questions. An author disclaimer: we have tried to be as comprehensive as possible and to describe technologies here in relation to the image. We are aware that we run the risk of oversimplifying as these technologies feed into one another – and comprise subcategories of each other. Alas, classifying these days remains to be the work of scholars and, increasingly, in collaboration with machines!

2.2.1 Machine Learning and ImageNet

In the 1950s artificial intelligence and, later, machine learning made similar inroads into text and image generations – precisely in relation to how systems are trained to see images. There were two ways in which machines or computers could see (Mitchell, 2020; cf Rettberg, 2023: 4). The first one is called *symbolic AI*: that particular strand is based upon how a form or a common sense could be explicitly coded as a set of rules or algorithms that a computer is programmed upon to think with. The second is *subsymbolic AI* and it is based upon machine learning from data: that is, a machine learning method where a computer program creates its own rules from patterns it finds in the data it is trained from. Up until the 1990s and before the advent of the Internet in mid-late 1990s, it seemed as if symbolic AI would be the future of computer vision; this was, however, not the case. The expansion of the Internet and digitisation of all sorts of datasets have made subsymbolic AI the norm instead. Subsymbolic AI – especially large language models and image recognition – continues to dominate, fueled by massive datasets and rapid advances in machine learning. Modern systems now integrate text, images, and audio, while quantum and edge AI further accelerate progress. Although symbolic methods are re-emerging through explainable and neuro-symbolic AI, the field is still primarily driven by subsymbolic approaches. Historically, image recognition was among the first machine learning applications, and that legacy continues as subsymbolic AI powers most state-of-the-art technologies in 2025.

In fact, the first machine learning technology was used for image recognition – 'the perceptron' and was concerned with reading hand-written numbers

(Rosenblatt, 1958: 286–408; Cf Rettberg, 2023: 5). A set of images was annotated/labelled by humans and then used to train an algorithm with 'neurons' meaning individual units that are given additional standard numeric values (0 and 1). Models were then trained on rounds of the same datasets – as a result this kind of machine learning was trained and able to identify an image it was trained on but it was not able to identify a random picture – even if the subject was the same. This machine learning technology was later replaced by deep learning – in the 1970s, where there is not a single layer of neurons but several and each layer is feeding its results to the next – thus making results more robust than with earlier machine learning. The key differences between the 1970s and now, beyond the availability of vastly more computing power and data, are the rise of neural networks and deep learning, the shift towards data-driven approaches, and the increased real-world applications of machine learning technology. In the early days of machine learning between the 1950s–1970s the focus was logical, knowledge-based algorithms. Since the 1970s significant changes have taken place beyond the increased computing power and data availability. The rise of neural networks and deep learning has really changed the landscape. In the 1980s there was a resurgence of interest in neural networks and backpropagation algorithms which were essential to train neural networks. Deep learning, a more advanced form of machine learning using neural networks with multiple layers, emerged in the 2010s and has enabled major breakthroughs in areas like computer vision, NLP, and autonomous systems. Advancements in powerful computing hardware (like GPUs) enabled the training of more complex deep learning models that were not feasible in the 1970s. A rough estimate of the amount of scientific effort put into AI and machine learning since the 1950s is shown in Figure 5.

In 2006, psychologist and computer scientist Geoffrey Hinton coined the term 'deep learning' to describe a revolutionary set of algorithms that enabled computers to recognize different types of objects and text characters in images and videos. This marked a significant breakthrough in the field of computer vision and image recognition. Building on Hinton's work, Fei-Fei Li started developing the ImageNet visual database in 2006. ImageNet became a catalyst for the AI boom, providing a comprehensive dataset that fuelled the development of increasingly sophisticated image recognition algorithms. The ImageNet dataset and the annual competition it spawned played a crucial role in driving rapid advancements in the field of computer vision. Thus, visuality and images play an important role in the recent history of AI development. The pioneering efforts by Hinton, Li, and others laid the foundation for the tremendous capabilities and potential we see today in image recognition and analysis. The combination of deep learning techniques and large-scale visual datasets has

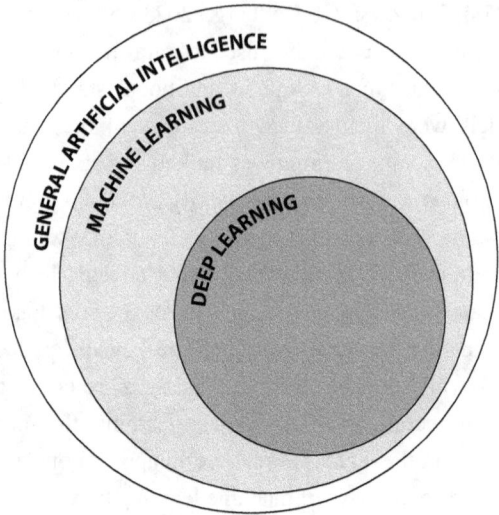

Figure 5 Estimate of scientific effort put into AI and machine learning since the 1950s. This figure presupposes a general field of AI outside machine learning and deep learning. This general category includes early AI disciplines (1950s to 1980s) such as expert systems, logic programming, robotics, search algorithms, NLP (pre-deep learning techniques), knowledge representation, and more. Machine learning expands from the mid-1980s to 2000s and deep learning emerges around 2010, now being prominent in research. Illustration: J. v. Bonsdorff.

transformed the way computers perceive and understand the world around us, opening up new possibilities in a wide range of applications, from autonomous vehicles to medical imaging and beyond.

In 1972 the now seminal article by Goldstein et al. (1972) set the grounds for the development of machine learning. It presented an interactive system that leverages both human and machine strengths to identify faces in photographs. Humans excel at detecting and describing distinctive facial features, while machines can make decisions based on accurate population statistics of stored face features. In experiments with 255 faces, the system narrowed down the population to the target individual in 99 per cent of trials using ten or fewer feature descriptions provided by humans. This demonstrated at the time the power of combining human perception with machine learning to efficiently identify faces. This experiment combined human facial feature detection as humans may easily spot unique, noteworthy features in a face and their ability to describe these features in natural language. These human capacities, combined with the fact that computers store population statistics on facial feature distributions, can rapidly match feature descriptions to stored face models and the

AI and Image

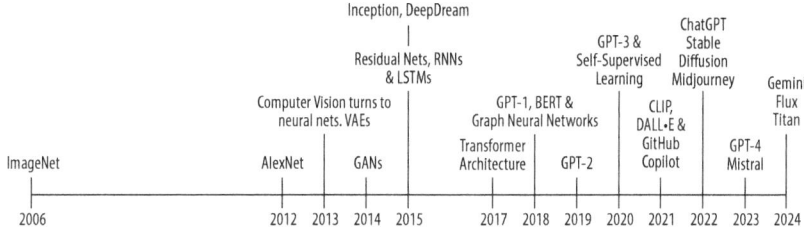

Figure 6 A timeline of landmarks for the technical development of computer vision 2006–2024. Illustration: J. v. Bonsdorff.

ability to narrow down to the most likely matches, provided the starting points for a machine-human collaboration on images. The human provides feature descriptions to the machine learning system, and the machine uses these to identify the most probable matching faces and the iteration between human and machine quickly converges on the target face. In summary, by integrating human and machine intelligence, the system achieves highly accurate and efficient face identification. The human's perceptual abilities complement the machine's statistical knowledge and rapid processing, resulting in a powerful interactive face recognition system.

From 1972 to this day the field of AI and its subsets have seen unprecedented development that is both fast paced as well as facilitated by the vast availability of training data. Let us return to the rapid technical development of computer vision techniques since ca. 2006 with the invention of ImageNet. In Figure 6 we provide a breakdown of stages of development in computer vision that have been important in relation to image analysis for art and heritage. It should be pointed out that this development goes in tandem with the development of NLP. We then identify some concrete uses in the field of computer vision and cultural heritage at each time period.

2.2.2 Deep Learning, Neural Networks, and Their Promise

Deep learning, as we noted earlier, is a type of machine learning that uses artificial neural networks to learn from large amounts of data. It is inspired by the structure and function of the human brain and is particularly effective at processing complex, unstructured data like images. Deep learning models for images typically use convolutional neural networks (CNNs). One early CNN was LeNet, created in 1998, designed to classify images of handwritten digits (LeCun et al., 1998). CNNs are designed to automatically learn features from the images, which makes them well-suited for tasks such as image classification, object detection, and image segmentation. Deep learning enables machines to learn complex visual representations from large amounts of image data, allowing them to classify, detect objects, and understand images with human-like accuracy. Its ability to automatically learn features makes it a powerful tool for computer vision applications. Deep learning is different from machine learning in that the data pre-processing by human experts that is typical in machine learning may be eliminated with deep learning. Deep learning can instead ingest and process unstructured data images, automating feature extraction, thus minimising the need of human experts. An example could be having a number of pictures of animals, such as pigs, donkeys, dogs and so on. Deep learning algorithms can determine features that may distinguish each animal from another (e.g. hooves or ears). In other machine learning, this hierarchy of features is established manually by a human expert.

From 2010 to 2017, ImageNet challenges (ImageNet Large Scale Visual Recognition Challenges; ILSVRC) were a driving force in the development particularly of advancing deep learning and neural networks for image recognition. Although CNNs had been around for some time (cf. LeNet above), it was not until 2012 that mainstream computer vision researchers paid attention to them (Murphy, 2022: 479). The turning point was the AlexNet convolutional neural network architecture presented during the ILSVRC 2012 contest, where it set a precedent for the field of Deep learning (Krizhevsky, Sutskever, & Hinton, 2012). In short, AlexNet presented solutions for handling large amounts of visual information, like the more than 14 million images in about 20,000 classes that ImageNet provided, thus reigniting interest in neural networks and computer vision. In the following years, similar architectures were presented, all deep convolutional neural networks, attaining even better results. From 2013, Variational Autoencoders (VAEs) and other architectures for more effective image processing were introduced (Kingma et al., 2014) – generative models that can learn to represent and generate data such as images and sounds. Variational autoencoders work by learning a compressed representation of the input data in a lower-dimensional space, a so-called *latent space*. New data are generated by sampling from this learned latent space. VAEs, later on, turned out to open up new avenues for generative modelling, useful with applications in fields like art and design. NEIL, the Never Ending Image Learner, was released also in 2013 to constantly collect, compare, and analyse semantic relationships between images, that is, how their meaning and significance are understood in relation (Chen, Shrivastava, & Gupta, 2013). NEIL used a combination of unsupervised and semi-supervised machine learning methods, including object and attribute recognition as well as scene classification.

The period 2014–2016 saw further expansion of AI capabilities regarding both computer vision and NLP. The winner of the 2015 ImageNet classification challenge was Kaiming. He and his team released a study called 'Deep Residual

Learning for Image Recognition', where they unveiled the design of residual neural networks, or *ResNets* (He et al., 2015). These architectures enhance information flow throughout the network by incorporating shortcut connections. Around the same time, significant advances were made in recurrent neural networks (RNNs) and long short-term memory (LSTM) models. Despite their 1990s origins, these models gained prominence around 2015 due to innovations like enhanced computational power and access to larger training datasets. Together with *ResNets*, these advancements enabled language models to better grasp text context and meaning, greatly enhancing language translation, text generation, and sentiment analysis. This progress laid the groundwork for current sophisticated *large language models*, LLMs (Dorfer, 2023).

DeepDream, introduced in 2015, is decidedly more artistic in its application than other models (Mordvintsev et al., 2015). Image features, learned by a network, also those only hinted at, can be amplified in variations of an input image. This iterative process highlights and exaggerates the features detected by the network, often resulting in highly intricate and hallucinogenic visual effects, resembling dream-like scenes. DeepDream uses the Inception CNN from the GoogLeNet model. The term used in Google's Inception modules for their neural network architecture was inspired by the movie *Inception* (2014), where the phrase 'We need to go deeper' referred to entering deeper levels of dreams within dreams (Murphy, 2022: 480 f., 494ff.).

2.2.3 Generative AI

Generative AI is a subset of artificial intelligence that uses machine learning algorithms to generate novel content based on patterns and examples from existing data, rather than simply analyse or act upon existing data like expert systems (see Figure 7). These models are able to generate information of

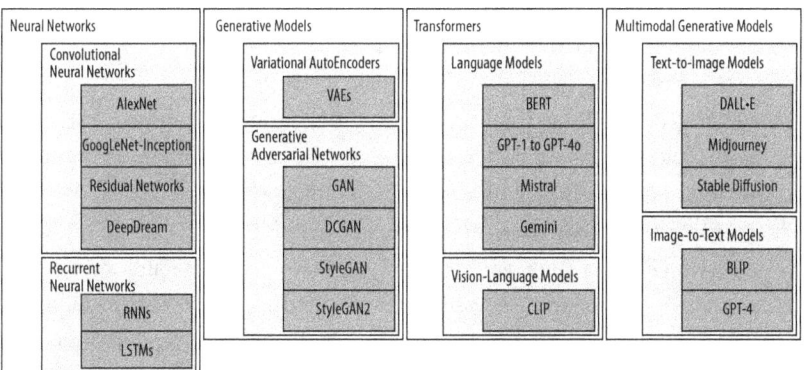

Figure 7 Types of AI algorithms and models categorised by primary functions and underlying technologies. Illustration: J. v. Bonsdorff.

the transformed input information or prompt (Gozalo-Brizuela & Garrido-Merchan, 2023). In the context of images, generative AI models can be trained on large datasets of artwork to autonomously create new images in a similar style. The history of Generative AI can be traced back to the 1950s, when researchers first began exploring the possibilities of artificial intelligence. In the 1950s, as we have seen previously in this Element, Frank Rosenblatt developed the Perceptron, an early neural network capable of being trained. This system laid the groundwork for future advances in machine learning. In 1961, Joseph Weizenbaum created ELIZA, an early chatbot that could respond to humans using natural language. ELIZA is considered one of the first historical examples of generative AI and has inspired controversy about the future of humanity in the age of the machines (Natale, 2019: 712–728). In the 1980s, neural networks gained popularity for generating new data. Geoffrey Hinton developed Boltzmann Machines that could generate data using interconnected nodes. In 2014, Ian Goodfellow introduced Generative Adversarial Networks (GANs), which quickly became a popular technique for generative AI. GANs consist of a generator and discriminator that work together to generate plausible new image data. Recent advances have been driven by large-scale neural networks and datasets. Key developments include ChatGPT for text generation, StyleGAN for high-quality image generation, and neural style transfer to apply artistic styles to images.

While generative AI at the time of writing this Element has a fairly short history, it has rapidly evolved from early chatbots to today's sophisticated language models and image generators. The field continues to advance, with exciting applications emerging across many industries. Some key applications of generative AI for images in art and heritage include generating novel artworks by learning the style and techniques of specific artists or art movements. This allows artists to explore new creative directions and ideas; restoring and completing damaged or unfinished artworks by predicting how the original artist may have completed the piece; producing images for use in art and heritage projects, such as visualising archaeological sites or architectural reconstructions; and generating synthetic training data to help improve computer vision models used for tasks like artwork classification and analysis.

Popular generative AI image models include Generative Adversarial Networks (GANs), which pit a generator network against a discriminator network to produce convincing images, as well as transformer-based models like DALL•E that generates images from text descriptions. These are used primarily in restoration processes for art and heritage artefacts (Atairu, 2024: 91–102; Cao et al., 2020: 1–14; Kumar & Gupta, 2023: 40967–40985). Transformer models are a type of deep learning architecture that has been adapted for computer vision tasks, such as image classification. Originally designed for sequence-to-sequence tasks like language translation, transformers use self-attention mechanisms to learn context and meaning by tracking relationships in sequential data. To apply transformers to images, the input image is first split into a sequence of flattened image discrete entities, called *patches*. 'Patches' in images correspond to 'tokens' in text. They both act as the fundamental units of input for the model. The patches are processed by the model to understand and generate predictions based on the input data. This sequence is then passed through the transformer model, which learns to understand the local and global features of the image. Transformer models are a powerful new approach for computer vision, adapting the self-attention mechanism to learn rich representations of images by analysing them as sequences of patches. While promising, there are still open challenges around architecture design, data efficiency, and interpretability.

The principal features and differences of transformers, generative AI and multimodal generative AI are the following (see Figure 7): transformers provide a reshaping of how models handle sequences and attention in both NLP and computer vision. Generative AI focuses on creating *new* content based on learned data patterns, with significant applications in generating convincing and creative digital content. Multimodal Generative AI, again, represents an integration of multiple data types, pushing the boundaries of how machines understand and create complex, context-rich content (cf. Section 3.2.1). Lately, the introduction in 2023 and 2024 of new AI tools like Mistral, Titan, and Flux has augmented the landscape of generative AI, since 2021 primarily belonging to Open AI and the later GPT family, as well as Midjourney and Stable Diffusion (both 2022). Mistral (2023) and Amazon's Titan (2024) focuses on making foundational AI models more accessible to developers and businesses. Flux (2024) by Black Forest Labs is an open-source alternative to Midjourney and Stable Diffusion, with an edge in text-to-video generation.

How does generative AI create an image from a textual prompt? In short, one can start with a prompt from a user: In our example we ask the AI to draw a flower pot (see Figure 8). In this way we initiate a text-to-image generation process. In the second stage, the AI breaks down the prompt into manageable tokens (cf. above) and converts these tokens into numerical vectors that capture their semantic meanings. After this, the AI utilises neural networks to understand the context and map the prompt into a so-called latent space. Latent space refers to a high-dimensional representation where the AI encodes all the possible attributes and relationships within the data, facilitating the identification and combination of features (flower, pot, drawing) that will appear in the generated image based on the input prompt. Subsequently, the image synthesis

Phase	Step	Description
Input phase	Prompt submission	A user submits a text prompt describing the desired image
Model interpretation	Tokenisation	The text prompt is broken down into tokens (words or pieces of words) that the machine can understand
	Embedding	Tokens are converted into numerical form (vectors) that encapsulate the semantic properties of the input
Processing generative model by the AI	Feature extraction, understanding content	Using layers of neural networks, especially transformers that can handle long-range dependencies, the AI analyses and understands the context of the prompt
	Latent space mapping	The AI maps the prompt into a high-dimensional space where similar concepts are near each other. This space represents potential features and styles that can appear in the final image
Image synthesis	Activation of generative components	Based on the learned data (during training) and the specific features identified from the prompt, the model activates its generative components
	Iterative refinement	The model may refine the generated image through multiple passes, adjusting details to better match the prompt
Output phase	Image rendering	The final image is rendered from the generative model's output
	Post-processing	Any necessary post-processing is applied to enhance image quality or ensure the image meets certain criteria (like resolution or colour correction)

Figure 8 Key components for text-to-image generation. These steps outline the journey from prompt submission to image output, illustrating an AI's capability to interpret textual descriptions and translate them into visual representations. Illustration: J. v. Bonsdorff.

starts: the generative components of the AI activate to construct the initial image, which is then refined again and again to align closely with the prompt's specifications. In the final output phase, the AI renders the final image (here, the flower pot) and applies any necessary post-processing to enhance quality and meet specific output criteria.

Generative AI as a form of synthetic conceptual art and culture has been examined from a number of perspectives. Computational formalism, understood also as the aesthetics of AI and its impact on visual cultural practices, has been extensively discussed (Manovich & Arielli, 2022; Wasielewski, 2023a). Understanding the computational nature of creativity, posthumanist scholarship argues for a deeper investigation of the socio-material complexity in implementing machines for creativity (Berry & Dieter, 2015; Hayles, 2017). As for now, generative AI (and especially its multimodal uses, cf. Section 3.2.1) seems to be the most rewarding area for creative solutions within the GLAM sector. However, the use of generative AI in art also raises questions around authorship, authenticity, and copyright. As technology continues to advance, it will be important for artists, museums, and policymakers to thoughtfully navigate the implications for the creative industries. Some of these implications for the implementation of AI technology for art and cultural heritage are discussed in the following section in detail.

3 Dystopian or Utopian Futures?

3.1 Dystopian Futures: Rage against the Machine?

So far we have seen the technology, the developments within AI technologies in relation to image, including success stories. In Section 3 we address the complexity of implementing AI while accounting for equality and diversity. In doing so, we focus thematically on a few umbrella issues, namely the question of bias and how it creeps into datasets, and point out situations in which generative AI technologies may be creating a misleading understanding of reality by creating synthetic yet seemingly realistic images. While we are not extensive here due to word economy, we hope that we at least inform our readers about the complexity of AI implementation for art and heritage datasets. For the same reasons, AI and its severe impact on climate change are simply mentioned in relation to further reading.

3.1.1 Bias, AI, and Image

Bias is widely recognised as any tendency or deviation in the processes of data collection, analysis, interpretation, and publication that may lead to incorrect conclusions, as noted by Gardenier and Resnik (2002: 65–74). Such biases can arise both deliberately and inadvertently. In the context of heritage collections, bias might manifest in seemingly simple ways, such as through the description of a photograph that inadvertently perpetuates societal prejudices related to race, ethnicity, age, gender, the LGBTQIA+ community, and disability. In the realm of computer vision applied to art cultural heritage, the issue of bias in training data has emerged as a significant concern, as discussed by Bagga and Piper (2020: 74–84). Specifically, when it comes to visual data, the impact of automated curation on the annotation of cultural heritage materials remains an area of uncertainty. A notable study examining the AI classification of Holocaust imagery by Makhortykh et al. (2021) underscores the potential dangers of misrepresentation, misattribution, trivialisation, or historical revisionism that may arise. This research points out that even the most sophisticated algorithms developed by leading technology companies like Google still face substantial challenges in accurately interpreting visual data.

Complexities almost always arise with the digital curation and management of images. This includes enriching metadata, organising information, and so on (see Prescott & Hughes, 2018, while Mallen and Park (2006) explore the varied methodologies institutions employ in the selection of items for digitisation within the British context). Globally, approaches to digitisation diverge significantly: for instance, the National Gallery in London might digitise its entire collection, whereas the British Library's Online Gallery might focus on digitising only its most sought-after items. Additionally, some collections are digitised based on thematic exhibitions or educational purposes, as seen with the Metropolitan Museum of Art in New York and the Swedish National Museum of Science and Technology (cited in Mallen & Park, 2006: 205–206; Foka, Attemark, & Wahlberg, 2022, respectively). This highlights that digitisation involves a complex selection process, further discussed by Ooghe et al. (2009). However, the selection process for digitisation is nuanced, influenced not only by the criteria set by those overseeing the selection but also by the digitisation tools and the subsequent digitalisation processes applied to cultural heritage materials. These tools, particularly when they are standard off-the-shelf solutions, may come with pre-existing biases in what to include or exclude and how to categorise the selected materials. This is especially problematic if the tools were initially trained on materials different from those they are applied to in the context of heritage collection digitisation. Thus, the process of digitisation and digitalisation introduces additional layers of selectivity, shaped by both human decisions and the capabilities and limitations of the technology used (see also Foka & Griffin, 2024: 6125–6136).

Additional complexities arise from questions of diversity and inclusion; art and cultural datasets, particularly concerning image, represent various cultures and diverse social groups inclusively, as emphasised by Risam in 2018. Heritage institutions have traditionally relied on cataloguing and labelling images and convey their rich histories and cultures to the public. Various factors, including the time period, ownership, acquisition history, museum history, location, the images themselves, and curatorial input, all contribute to a dynamic interaction between individuals and information, as discussed by Macdonald in 2011. The origins of many collections, often acquired through discoveries, excavations, expeditions, or even appropriation by colonisers, mean that narratives of colonisation and oppression are intrinsically linked to these analogue artistic and cultural records, even if not explicitly stated. The field of critical cultural heritage research is increasingly focused on revising and improving these records. It seeks to establish heritage as a contemporary construct, viewing it as a past practice that is being reconstructed in the present. This perspective is supported by the works of Smith (2006), Emerick (2014), Harrison (2013), and Silverman, Waterton, and Watson (2017). Critical heritage studies delve into the relationship between people, heritage, and societal power, challenging the conventional discourse on heritage. According to Smith (2006), Smith, Shackel, and Campbell (2012), and Logan and Wijesuriya (2015), heritage is seen as a process shaped by socio-political dynamics that reflect the power structures within society. Art and media cultures can also be critical in the same way especially in relation to the depictions of individuals and cultural milieus – especially postcolonial approaches (Bharathi Larsson, 2016).

The fields of art and cultural heritage increasingly lean on predictive models that are tasked with interpreting and categorising human memories and their physical manifestations. In this context, interpretation involves the creation of authoritative narratives and categorisations that serve both academic research and curatorial endeavours. Traditionally, these critical decisions have been the purview of highly educated individuals exercising their best judgement. However, machines are playing a growing role in these processes. Because of the growing machine integration, the oversight and nuanced judgement of human experts remain crucial to guide and to correct potential inaccuracies in these automated processes. The effectiveness of such decision-making is closely linked to the quality of the underlying data and the criteria used for categorisation. Given the ubiquitous nature of bias within cultural heritage collections we hereby similarly address the challenges posed by the integration of machine or computer-based interpretations and predictions. It is also worth noting that heritage collections are extensive and diverse, encompassing a variety of materials and content types. The selection of machine learning tools is inherently dependent on the nature of the data and the specific insights sought from it. For example, while algorithms developed for analysing mediaeval manuscripts to recognize handwritten text may be valuable, they may not be directly applicable to tasks like classifying expressionist paintings (Foka et al., 2023).

Scholarly analysis has delved into the emerging concept of algorithmic culture, which is characterised by the sorting, classification, and ranking of individuals, locations, objects, and concepts (Striphas, 2015; 396): a quantification of culture of sorts. The concerns about AI accentuating racial and gender discrimination are particularly pertinent in the context of computer vision. This technology, which enables machines to interpret and act upon visual data, has been criticised for reinforcing biases present in the data it is trained on (Benjamin, 2019; Buolamwini & Gebru, 2018; Chun, 2021). Such biases can lead to discriminatory practices, affecting marginalised groups disproportionately.

Scholarly research on AI technology underscores that bias is an unintended consequence arising from various decisions and practices within the AI development process (Fahse, 2021). For instance, studies on facial recognition and classification highlight bias as a disparity in classification accuracy across different demographic groups, thereby favouring some groups over others (Angileri, 2019; Du, 2020). Another perspective views bias as decisions disproportionately favouring a specific group (Van Giffen, 2022). Across both critical heritage and AI discussions, bias is perceived as a detrimental outcome where an algorithm disproportionately benefits or performs better for certain groups within a dataset. Further research into digital cultural data reveals how bias transitions from collections to datasets and then to platforms. Biases within museum collections can manifest in the datasets, databases, and aggregators that increasingly employ AI technologies like machine learning (Huster, 2013; Kizhner et al., 2021). Kizhner et al. (2021) discuss the bias in the cultural heritage platform Google Arts and Culture, noting that the choices behind digitisation, publication, aggregation, and promotion often obscure the limitations of institutional, social, and political frameworks. They advocate for making these epistemic choices transparent, documented, and interpretable.

Bias in image collections also encompasses issues of digital cultural colonialism and otherness, a tension between contrasting structures such as European/western versus other, North versus South, and national centre versus periphery (Caton & Santos, 2008; Said, 1978; Salazar, 2012; Sharp, 2002; Risam, 2018). This tension extends to gender, challenging binary classifications. Dominant community epistemologies are often promoted in national cultural heritage collections and digital aggregators, perpetuating a 'status quo at scale' (Kizhner et al., 2021). Gender-based othering, for example, has led to misclassifications in eighteenth-century Swedish portraits, where men were identified as women due to long hair and jewellery. The selective nature of digitisation further illustrates bias (Argyriou et al., 2020). As Davis et al. (2021) succinctly put it, 'algorithms are animated by data, data come from people, people make up society, and society is unequal.' Acknowledging this chain of inequality, there have been numerous efforts to address biases in AI, particularly in the context of cultural heritage. Davis et al. (2021) discuss algorithmic reparation and intersectionality as frameworks to combat structural inequalities reflected and amplified by machine learning outcomes. They highlight the importance of recognising the differential exposure to discrimination among diverse groups and the challenges of addressing biases in AI systems, including social, legal, and institutional barriers.

Even in the realm of computer vision, biases related to digital cultural colonialism and dominant epistemologies persist, leading to biased representations of knowledge (De Souza Santos, 2018; Milan & Trere, 2019). To avoid merely replicating biases, AI technology must evolve to embrace complex, non-binary, and non-dominant interpretations. The critical perspectives from the humanities and social sciences, therefore, play a vital role in highlighting these issues and advocating for more inclusive and equitable AI development practices. The critical perspectives on AI from the humanities and social sciences, increasingly supported by scholars in computer science, emphasise the need for ethical, responsible AI development. These perspectives highlight the importance of addressing racial and gender discrimination, among other social and ethical concerns, to ensure that AI technologies benefit all members of society equitably. Researchers are called to step into the role of 'active enactors', who shape algorithms through their scholarly work – as algorithms are cultural because 'they are composed of collective human practices' (Seaver, 2017: 5). Scholars in the field of digital humanities have wrestled with their identity as active enactors for many years, initially concentrating on collaborations with museums, libraries, and archives to explore past cultures and create digital replicas (O'Sullivan, 2023; Schreibman et al., 2008). Moreover, they have delved deeper into the realms of new media, the Internet, and its diverse cultures, often analysing the digital footprints left behind (Blanke & Prescott, 2016; Grandjean, 2016; Manovich, 2011; Rogers, 2013).

We contend that bias may be a constant in cultural datasets, and thus AI systems might replicate or even exacerbate it. Thus, it is crucial to explore and propose avenues for enhanced collaboration among various stakeholders (including professionals, subject matter experts, and technical specialists) to develop effective bias mitigation strategies. The allure of being able to categorise large volumes of image data is undeniable. However, it is crucial to consider the implications for the quality of metadata and the potential for AI bias, especially when dealing with sensitive and historically significant content that may carry political and cultural controversies. In yet another important strand of research, efforts have been made to understand the conditions and specific ontological and epistemological status of AI, and how inherent technical features of such systems might lead to bias (Offert and Bell, 2021). As has been pointed out in the context of critical AI research, bias is always present in the training and deployment of AI models (Davis et al., 2021). Machine learning algorithms produced using cultural data tend to reproduce cultural bias, replicating or even amplifying existing relations of power and marginalisation (Barocas et al., 2023; Broussard, 2018; Ciecko, 2020). While critical AI research has extensively pointed out the problems of bias and amplification of cultural patterns, the potential of using bias as an explorative (probing) technique for identifying and visualising such patterns is yet underexplored. Also using algorithms on data can help identify biases in data, which were invisible otherwise

We finally ought to stress that bias, and particularly racial or gender bias spans both technical and epistemological realms, involving the gender binary's role as a deeply racialised instrument of colonial dominance and control. Recent scholarly work has introduced the concept of auto-essentialization (Scheuerman, Pape, & Hanna, 2021), which refers to the application of automated technologies to reinforce foundational distinctions of identity that originated during colonial times. This process is examined through the lens of historical gender embodiment practices, including the normalisation of the European gender binary through disciplines like sexology, physiognomy, and phrenology throughout the nineteenth and twentieth centuries. These practices are seen as precursors to modern automated facial analysis technologies in computer vision, highlighting the need for a critical reevaluation of AI/ML applications in image recognition as contemporary manifestations of much older technological concepts (Scheuerman, Pape, & Hanna, 2021). It is crucial to acknowledge that these systems are designed to identify features by focusing on elements within images that are recognisable to humans, potentially perpetuating human biases (Banerjee et al., 2021). It is finally assumed that machine learning has a normalising effect in identifying faces and postures especially when it comes to how it aims to 'ameliorate them' by adjusting properties – especially in applications such as social media filters (Rettberg, 2023: 118–127)

If AI implementation such as computer vision technology is applied thoughtfully, it holds the potential to foreground significant issues for heritage collections, especially those comprising images. The challenge lies in moving beyond the conventional technological framework that relies on the premise of categorising images through clear-cut, machine-generated keywords. This approach faces inherent difficulties, particularly with visual art, which inherently defies simplistic and fixed interpretations. To leverage image recognition technology in a way that enhances interpretive depth, it is imperative to develop systems capable of accommodating complex, nuanced, and non-stereotypical analyses.

3.1.2 Generative Art, Synthetic Images: Forgery, Deepfakes, and Propaganda

In 'Midjourney Can't Count: Questions of Representation and Meaning for Text-to-Image Generators', Wasielewski (2023b: 71–82) delves into the challenges and peculiarities of AI-driven text-to-image generation tools like DALL·E, Midjourney, and Stable Diffusion. The discussion is centred on two primary issues: the representation of human hands and the broader problem of counting objects within generated images. There are strengths and weaknesses in generative AI and image: the release of text-to-image generation tools in 2022 democratised access to AI capabilities, allowing a wide range of users to create images from text prompts. This accessibility has led to a surge in creative outputs and a vibrant community of users sharing their creations and tips online. These tools have shown remarkable ability to generate imaginative and fantastical scenes, such as an astronaut riding a horse on the moon. This capability underscores the potential for AI to assist in creative processes by producing unique and visually compelling images that might be difficult or time-consuming to create manually. Efforts have been made to address biases in the training data, such as ensuring diversity in the depiction of people in generated images. For instance, Wasielewski brings up an example that DALL·E has been updated to generate a diverse array of individuals when prompted with terms like CEO (i.e Chief Executive Officer), reflecting a more inclusive representation.

However, Wasielewski further discusses that one of the most well-known issues with text-to-image generators is their difficulty in accurately rendering human hands; she argues that these AI models do not truly understand the objects they depict. They can replicate visual forms based on training data but lack the experiential and contextual knowledge that humans possess. This limitation is evident in their inability to accurately interpret prompts that require a deeper understanding of the physical world, such as the correct depiction of hands or the accurate counting of objects. The AI's approach to image generation is thus described as computational formalism, where the focus is on replicating visual patterns without understanding the underlying meaning. This results in images that may look superficially correct but lack the nuanced understanding that comes from real-world experience and context (cf. discussion on 'precision models' in Section 3.2.2). As these technologies continue to evolve, addressing these fundamental weaknesses will be crucial for their development and more effective integration into creative and practical applications. Berryman (2024) explores the intersection of art history and AI technology, focusing on Generative Adversarial Networks (GANs). It critiques the use of GANs in creating art, arguing that their reliance on style autonomy reinstates a formalist view of art history and perpetuates a narrow, style-centric 'historical modernism'.

With synthetic images, however, come additional issues, beyond limitations that are posed by machine assumptions of formalism, creativity, style and novelty. One example is the Deepfakes, a form of synthetic media created through AI/ML technologies, offering a dual-edged sword in terms of personalised engagement. These technologies have the capability to modify and transform sounds or images, presenting both opportunities and challenges (Kwok & Koh, 2021: 1798–1802). On the one hand, deepfakes have the power to revitalise historical events and figures, offering a new dimension to cultural experiences. This is exemplified by the Dalí Museum's innovative use of deepfake technology to bring Salvador Dalí back to life, alongside similar initiatives at the Munch Museum and the Johannes Larsen Museum (Benford et al., 2022: 1–16; Lee, 2019). On the other hand, deepfakes have found a place in popular culture, with applications like Wombo.ai enabling users to animate their selfies in harmony with music. These uses highlight the potential of deepfakes to create immersive and entertaining interactions with art, providing professionals and general users alike with advanced tools for media manipulation. This contributes to the expanding remix culture, allowing for the creative repurposing of media (Broca, 2010: 121–123).

The emergence of generative models like ChatGPT and the creation of synthetic imagery through DALL·E have captured the public's imagination, yet the cultural and creative sectors are increasingly turning to predictive models. These models are adept at analysing and categorising human memories and their manifestations. Such interpretations often draw from established narratives and classifications, reflecting the biases inherent in historical curatorial practices. Traditionally, these evaluative tasks were the domain of highly educated individuals. However, machines are now playing a significant role in this process. The effectiveness of these decisions is deeply linked to the data quality and the criteria used for categorisation. Through AI, the realms of art and culture are navigating new pathways, and are blurring the lines between authenticity and fabrication, truth and falsehood, especially in the era of advanced deepfakes. While truth may be in jeopardy, AI also holds the promise of transforming our understanding of the human experience. Machine learning, powered by extensive datasets, enables technologies like DALL·E and ChatGPT to generate synthetic images that, despite being artificial, possess

AI and Image 49

a semblance of plausibility and authenticity. In essence, these technologies are not merely documenting art and culture but are actively creating it. The ethical implications are significant, given the prevalent use of AI in spreading computational propaganda and misinformation.

Conversely, the application of deepfakes raises important considerations around trust and ethical use, as it involves sophisticated biometric techniques. It emphasises the need for building trust, engaging stakeholders, and adopting participatory design approaches. Employing AI-generated avatars for storytelling opens new avenues for heritage enthusiasts and museum visitors, offering fresh perspectives on society, democracy, and humanity. Deepfake artworks serve as both a medium and a message, capable of conveying impactful narratives. However, the dissemination of deepfakes is intrinsically linked to the internet, relying on a symbiotic relationship for their spread. This dual nature of deepfakes underscores the importance of responsible use and the potential for innovative applications in cultural and entertainment contexts (see Foka et al., 2023: 815–825). N. Katherine Hayles' posthumanist perspective emphasises the material and embodied complexity across various cultural fields, including AI (Hayles, 2017). The concepts of the postdigital, which advocate for a processual and ecological approach to culture and creativity, are also pertinent (Berry & Dieter, 2015).

Are all synthetic images capable of misinformation? Some images created by humans and their AI identification, classification and rendering generate new scholarly inquiry. Generative models are presented by new technologies such as, for example, the production of synthetic images using word description with programs such as DALL·E, Stable Diffusion and so on, but often the process of identification and classification of predictive models that focus on interpreting and classifying human memory and its artefacts are not trained on specialised datasets. Interpretation is, in this case, related to creating authoritative accounts and classifications by training an algorithm. The quality of the algorithm and its interpretation is dependent on the quality of the data and collective human expertise in curating, preparing, and selecting the description for these datasets. For example, we might ask DALL·E to prepare an image of an archaic Kore (see Figure 10). An expert in art history and the ancient Mediterranean would know that Archaic Korai are ancient Greek sculptures depicting young women, characterised by their upright posture, detailed drapery, and the iconic archaic smile. (Made primarily from marble, these figures were often painted and served as votive offerings or grave markers.) Unlike the nude, male kouroi, korai are clothed, reflecting contemporary fashion and craftsmanship. Their function and representation vary, with some believed to depict goddesses. Some notable examples include the Peplos Kore and Phrasikleia Kore (see Figure 9; Smith & Plantzos, 2018; for a visual representation of the peplos Kore see https://www

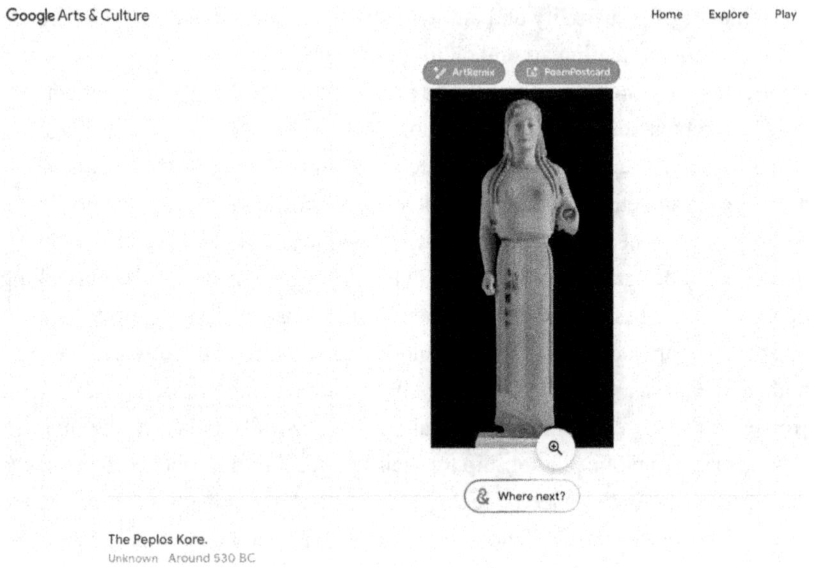

Figure 9 A Screenshot of Google Arts and Culture depicting the Peplos Kore.

Figure 10 DALL·E 2 2023 generative art created with the prompt: 'a photorealistic image of an archaic Kore'. This image does not correspond to reality.

.classics.cam.ac.uk/museum/collections/peplos-kore). Now if we prompt a generative AI platform, for example, DALL·E, it is not entirely certain that the generated image will actually be able to encapsulate the form or the aesthetics of an actual archaic Kore (see Figure 10). It is possible to generate variations on the image and vary the prompts to reach a satisfying level of Kore-ness that, say, an archaeologist or a classical art scholar would approve of. This takes a lot of work and, again, a vast repository of research and deep factual and connoisseurial insights in the field – most likely in the possession of a small number of human experts. Human input, curating, and fine-honing the output is the only possible solution for teaching AI tools high-level cultural competence.

As of the time of writing this Element (2024), there has been major updates to DALL·E and DALL·E 2. The company stated that they are no longer allowing new users to DALL·E 2. DALL·E 3 has higher quality images, improved prompt adherence, and they have started rolling out image editing. These are services available after subscription via ChatGPT Plus, Team and Enterprise and the OpenAI API.

Deepfake technology, which leverages artificial intelligence to create plausible digital impersonations, has been applied in various ways across art, culture, and propaganda. Its use spans from reimagining famous artworks to serving as a tool for political misinformation.

In the realm of art and culture, deepfake technology has breathed new life into classic art. For instance, the Mona Lisa has been animated to talk and move as though she were a real person, offering a novel way to engage with this iconic piece. Artists Bill Posters and Daniel Howe took this a step further with their immersive installation Spectre, which included deepfake videos of celebrities like Mark Zuckerberg and Kim Kardashian speaking on topics they never actually discussed (https://billposters.ch/the-zuckerberg-deepfake-heard-around-the-world/). This project aimed to highlight the challenges of discerning truth in the digital age. Furthermore, museums are exploring the use of deepfake technology to animate paintings or portraits of historical figures (sometimes called 'deep nostalgia'), potentially revolutionising the visitor experience by providing interactive and personalised engagements.

However, it is important to note that the use of deepfakes extends beyond artistic expression into the realm of propaganda. Russia, for example, has employed deepfake technology to create videos with anti-Moscow rhetoric, aiming to influence public consciousness. A notable instance involved a deepfake video of Valeriy Zaluzhnyi, Commander-in-Chief of Ukraine's Armed Forces, making false statements to incite unrest. Additionally, following the death of Vladimir Zhirinovsky, leader of the Russian Liberal Democratic Party of Russia (LDPR), deepfake technology was used to maintain his influence. A Telegram channel called NeuroZhirinovsky generates audio files in Zhirinovsky's voice, answering voters' questions and producing messages aligned with Kremlin rhetoric (see more in Samoilenko & Suvorova, 2023: 507–529). These examples underscore the dual nature of deepfake technology. While it offers innovative avenues for artistic expression and cultural engagement, its use in propaganda highlights significant ethical concerns. The ability to spread misinformation and influence public opinion with realistic impersonations poses challenges to democratic values and security, emphasising the need for critical scrutiny and regulatory measures.

Finally, we would like to address how scholars have been discussing the fact that AI methods and tools for image are actually challenging the notion of authenticity altogether. Wasielewski (2023c: 191–201) argues that low-resolution images, often considered poor images as per Hito Steyerl's definition, are particularly valuable in AI applications because they limit unnecessary detail, or noise, which can hinder machine analysis. This is a significant departure from traditional views that equate higher resolution and more detail with better quality and authenticity. Concerning questions of authenticity, Wasielewski explores how deep learning systems, which analyse images at the pixel level, often use down-sampled images to improve the efficiency and accuracy of object recognition tasks (cf. our discussion on 'patches'). These systems are trained on large datasets of low-resolution images, which are easier to process and more effective for identifying patterns and features necessary for tasks like facial recognition, medical imaging, and automated art authentication. In doing so, Wasielewski challenges Walter Benjamin's notion of authenticity, which is tied to the 'here and now' of the original artwork. In the digital age, authenticity is increasingly derived from the formal properties of digital images and their reproducibility. AI systems do not perceive images as humans do; they process them as quantifiable data, focusing on pixel patterns rather than the overall aesthetic or material qualities of the image. This shift suggests a new model of authenticity that emerges from the data itself, rather than from the unique aura of an original work. Wasielewski very correctly highlights the ethical and practical implications of this shift. For instance, the reliance on crowdsourced labour for labelling training data raises questions about the ethics of such practices. Moreover, the indiscriminate nature of machine vision, which does not differentiate between foreground and background or incidental details, can lead to misclassifications and a fragmented understanding of images. AI and deep learning are thus redefining authenticity in image analysis by prioritising the functional, quantitative aspects of digital images over their qualitative, aesthetic properties. This new form of authenticity is indeed rooted in the reproducibility and data-driven nature of digital images, challenging traditional notions tied to the physical presence and uniqueness of original artworks.

3.2 Utopian Promises

3.2.1 Possibilities of Large Multimodal Foundation Models

We hereby have been focusing on images – yet AI is essentially multimodal. Multimodal AI refers to systems that can process and integrate multiple types of data inputs, such as text, images, audio, and video, to produce more accurate and sophisticated outputs. This contrasts with unimodal AI, which processes only one type of data. Multimodal AI systems are designed to recognize patterns and connections between different data types, making their outputs more compelling and intuitive. Examples include OpenAI's GPT-4 V(ision), which can process both text and images, and other systems that combine video, audio, and text for various applications. Gunther Kress emphasises that the world of meaning has always been multimodal and calls for a theoretical framework for literacy and multimodality (Kress 2010, 174; Kress, 2003, 35ff.).

Artistic and cultural images oscillate between modes and are also multimodal. In antiquity, the description of a picture has been labelled *ekphrasis*. Ekphrasis is fundamentally a form of descriptive speech that aims to bring the subject vividly before the eyes of the audience. This vividness, or *enargeia*, is a crucial element, making the description so clear and detailed that it almost allows the audience to see the object through words. A prime example of ekphrasis is Philostratos' *Eikones* which vividly describes sixty-four paintings in a Neapolitan villa. In a sense it is a verbal analysis, a *transduction*, that is, how to package similar meanings but in different modes. In the case of *ekphrasis*, this would be translating visual data into verbal data. Lev Manovich refers to an additional mode with the term *transcoding*: that is, navigating between two communicating layers in the digital image: the cultural layer and the computer layer, each affecting another: The cultural layer of a digitised image, what is seen on the screen, is comparable to an image in any form, and the computer layer, the code, works in the realm of processing data (Manovich, 2001, 45ff.).

Putting together ekphrastic texts through images may be defined as a core task of interpretive practice: pointing out features of the image in text form leads to further finds of similar images that have to be described in text and so forth. This process of oscillation between modal stages may lead to new and more differentiated knowledge. The interpreter stands on two ladders at the same time, one textual and one visual; this wrestling between modalities excites richer interpretations. This we coin as *multimodal reasoning*. Sam Rose outlines a similar approach to art interpretation, emphasising the importance of both textual and visual analysis. He suggests that interpretation involves a dynamic process of moving from encountering an unfamiliar (visual) object to making sense of it through description and (textual) contextualization (cf. Rose, 2022).

Multimodal reasoning is abundant especially in the demonstrative setting of the pedagogue. Take for example the endeavours of Axel Gauffin, curator at Nationalmuseum (Swedish for the National Museum of Art) in Stockholm. From 1917 onwards, Gauffin worked for an ambitious and groundbreaking filmatic documentation of highlights at the Nationalmuseum in Stockholm

(Ehrenborg, 1956). Only a few films were produced and only traces still exist. One of these pedagogical experiments is a documentary of the large equestrian statue of St. George in Storkyrkan in Stockholm from 1489 (see Figure 14). The film from 1919 is listed by UNESCO's catalogue on art films from 1949 as the earliest known example of a film with focus on the fine arts (Unesco, 1949: 68). The art historian Johnny Roosval, who appears in the film, took part in a grand restoration of the polychrome wooden sculptures. It seems the silent movie was supposed to be presented together with a text read aloud, now lost, since Roosval, in different scenes, points to a series of features of the sculpture that he wants to explain (see Figure 11). Thus, we are confronted with an act of multimodal demonstration in the sense of Kress and van Leeuwen's communicative functions (Kress & van Leeuwen, 2021: 16 f.): We encounter *representations* of the art work itself, *compositional* guidance (how the objects-to-be-explained are arranged), and *interactive* features (how the demonstrator Roosval engages the audience through gestures and a spoken script).

Thus, multimodal reasoning as a pedagogical tool is a common trait in scholarly tradition. We may add the reservation that multimodality may not

Figure 11 Multimodal reasoning: In the world's first film on art from 1919, art historian Johnny Roosval points out features on the large mediaeval equestrian wooden sculpture of St. George in Storkyrkan, Stockholm. Still from the film *S:t Göran och draken* (1919). KB SF2415.

always be a conscious choice when teaching or researching. Well-established boundaries between the disciplines often lead to a unimodal way of thinking: For literary scholars the text applies, for film scholars the film, for art historians the visual arts. Through the works of Kress, van Leeuwen, Grusin, Macken-Horarik, Manovich, and others we learn that adopting a multimodal approach by integrating various forms of media into research and analysis leads to cross fertilisation between domains and more differentiated insights (Grusin, 1999: Macken-Horarik, 2016: Manovich, 2001).

Now, in the world of artificial intelligence (AI), large multimodal models are emerging. These do not simply understand unimodal modes like text, images, audio and video but are also able to link these modalities together (see Figure 12). We would like to delve into how the integration of these multimodal AI systems could be used for the cultural heritage field. There is a burgeoning interest in multimodal deep learning (sometimes MMDL; Jabeen et al., 2023). Models such as Contrastive Language Image Pre-training (CLIP, see Figure 7), trained on paired images and texts, can be applied to a wide range of text-to-image, image-to-image, and image-to-text prediction tasks. One multimodal connection is already within reach of utmost importance for the Cultural

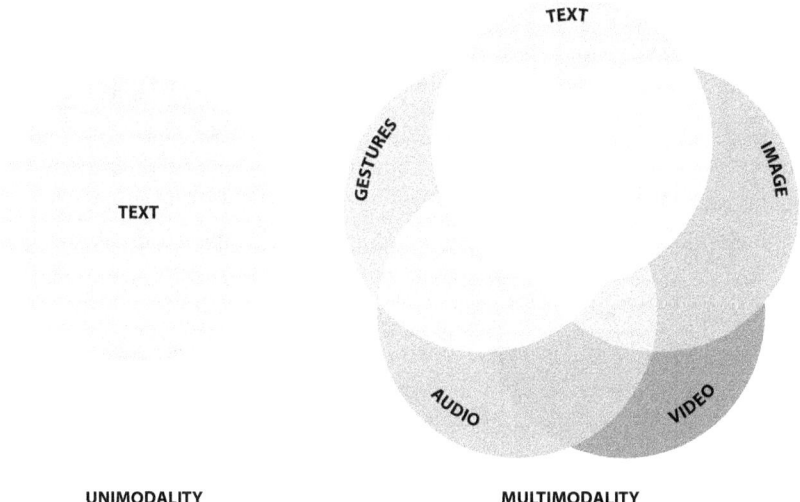

Figure 12 The difference between unimodality (or monomodality) and multimodality. Unimodality implies one clear mode of communication (e.g. 'text'). Multimodality integrates different modes (e.g. 'text', 'image', etc.), implying a richness of communication (but possibly a loss of clarity). Even if many modes may signify the same thing, they never fully overlap. Illustration: J. v. Bonsdorff.

Heritage sector – automatic image description through image-to-text algorithms through GPT-4 in 2023 and subsequent solutions. Automatic annotations have been a significant focus since the advent of Microsoft's and Google's captioning devices in 2017 and 2018, respectively (Sharma et al., 2018). Additionally, the integration of automatic annotation capabilities in smartphones has further popularised this technology, allowing users to label and organise their photos. The trend underscores the growing importance of automated systems in managing and enriching digital content from cultural heritage collections, making handling easier as well as the results more accessible across various domains.

A few digital humanities scholars have recognised such machine learning models as extremely useful for exploring and analysing image-text combinations at scale and in the context of cultural heritage. Smits and Wevers explore the integration of multimodal tools, particularly focusing on the use of contrastive machine learning models to handle digital visual historical collections (Smits & Wevers, 2023). They discuss different methodological approaches that have been applied to various media, including photography and magic lantern slides. These approaches aim to provide a comprehensive understanding of the multimodal characteristics of the artefacts. They also emphasise multimodal integration of various computational techniques when exploring the varied and large volumes of data one encounters in digital visuals in cultural heritage collections. Smits and Wevers reference the distant viewing framework proposed by Arnold and Tilton, which is used to analyse visual and multimodal materials (Arnold & Tilton, 2019). This framework allows researchers to gain insights from large datasets by focusing on formal properties such as texture, colour, and shape. Smits and Wevers highlight the key concern of ensuring that the information stored in multimodal corpora is accessible. The authors discuss the importance of developing annotation frameworks that can identify, categorise, and describe units of analysis and their interrelations. The integration of multimodal tools have clearly positive implications for cultural heritage: by leveraging these tools in connection with historical collections, researchers and curators can uncover new connections and insights that were previously inaccessible, revealing connections between different forms of information or modalities and thus open up new creative research perspectives.

Interestingly enough, most of these tools are – still – *bimodal*, or rely on only two modalities: text and image. When speaking of multimodality, one would expect more modalities such as audio, video, and tactile data, beyond just text and image. So, what would be the purpose of a large multimodal model? The relevance of such multimodal models for the humanities can hardly be overestimated. They could serve as catalytic tools that generate new ideas and act as a driver for innovative research approaches. It is conceivable to develop a multimodal database that not only reflects content from different media but also enables deep insights into the relationship between these media. Such a database could include analysis of paintings, sculptures, music, film, and more, each enriched with rich metadata to enable precise search and analysis.

How would this work? Without getting entangled in technicalities: In order to cope with the diversity and complexity of different types of media in the humanities, multimodal models require advanced algorithms, high computing power, and media-savvy expertise. Think of modalities as different types of input or information, like text, images, or sounds. Imagine converting (or mapping) these types of information into small, distinct pieces, like turning a picture into a collection of tiny dots (pixels) or breaking down a sentence into individual words or letters. These distinct pieces, as we have explained earlier, are called *tokens*. Each type of input, for example, text or images, has its own special way, that is, tool to break it down into these small pieces. For text, this tool might break sentences into words; for images, it might break pictures into pixels or patches. Thus, the tools making the tokens have to be modality-specific. The really creative part is that the AI can take any combination of these pieces or tokens (whether they come from text, images, or sounds) and use them to create new text, new images, or new sounds. Alternatively, machine learning can be used to search for texts, images, and sounds carrying similar meanings, so-called cross-domain metaphors: This would be the lexicon function, which we turn to now.

As a thought experiment, we would like to introduce the possibility of *the truly multimodal lexicon* (see Figure 13). Traditional lexica and encyclopaedia are based on keywords in text. Cross-modal connections are limited –

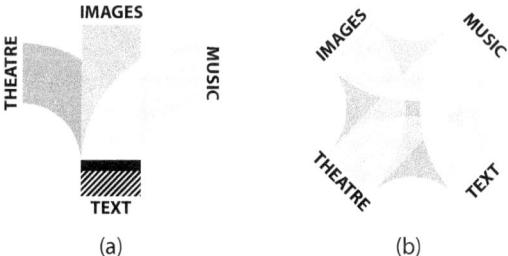

Figure 13 A comparison between a customary bimodal lexicon and a possible multimodal lexicon. (a) Depicts the traditional lexicon, where the root consists of textual head words. (b) Depicts a truly multimodal (or cross-modal) lexicon, where any modality can serve as an entry. Search terms can be formulated in other modalities than text. Cross-connections between all modalities are possible. Illustration: J. v. Bonsdorff.

with the obvious exception of illustrated encyclopaedia at least since Diderot's *Encyclopédie*. If one would like to find for example a musical topos (a 'mood') in a theatrical setting, one needs several lexica: one for looking up the musical topos, and at several ones for uses of mood in dramatic texts, staging, and gestics. How would a multimodal lexicon help? It would allow humanities researchers and GLAM professionals to link and analyse diverse forms of data (text, images, audio, etc.) in a unified framework, enabling deeper insights and uncovering connections across different media. This would enhance the interpretation, preservation, and presentation of cultural artefacts, making them more accessible and comprehensible to the public. A multimodal lexicon would not make the textual entry or prompt totally superfluous, but possible to combine with sound and visuals of a performance. In a sense, a multimodal lexicon would be *symmetrical*: not logocentric, not just visual but putting more of our sensory input and medial experiences into play: this would speed up and maximise the interchange of the *shareable* in the cultural heritage context (cf. Giugliano & Laudante, 2020). As shown in Figure 13, most lexica use text as a prime root; the 'head words' or 'entries' used for localising a subject. In a truly multimodal lexicon, any input in any mode would serve as an entry. Further, multimodal models are superior to unimodal, mostly linguistic models, because they support a wider range of tasks and are more consistent with the human ability to live in a world that relies on multisensory input. We would like to refer to Hans Belting's image model once again: people literally produce sensory sceneries through their memories and dreams – the brain itself serves as a living medium. Thus, the sensory-boosted lexicon seems close to the multimodal reasoning with which we started this section.

Some areas lend themselves more easily to the shareable. Spitzer talks about cross-domain metaphors that bridge over historical culture, as opposed to likenesses within a unimodal system (Spitzer, 2004: 54–56: von Bonsdorff, 2019). Usually, such metaphors, along with imagery, motifs, allegories, personifications, moods, and many more, are handled by mostly uni- or bimodal lexica. A properly curated, rich latent space covering such subjects could couple such cross-domain features in an effective way. The development of a truly multimodal lexicon is supported by current research in cross-modal information retrieval (sometimes just IR) and multimodal AI Titles on articles like 'Recognizing Everything from All Modalities at Once' or 'Any-to-Any' modal models are common (Bachmann, 2024; Zhang, 2024). Different types of information, like text, images, and sounds can be integrated in a common representation space, which is like having a shared language or a common way to represent the different types. In this way, the information from different media sources can be easily compared, even if they appear different (like matching a word to a picture that represents that word). This is called semantic matching. The matching can only be done when certain features remain consistent across different types of information: the features must be modality-invariant. The integration of various modalities into a common representation space, along with advanced semantic matching and modality-invariant features, can enable new creative research perspectives and uncover unrecognised connections between different forms of information. We started this section with an example of multimodal reasoning – the pedagogical use of film in explaining a mediaeval wooden sculpture. In the case of museum collections, a search tool able to make connections between different information domains would be invaluable for creating new ways of explaining collection content. Multimodal search engines would facilitate such idea- and content-driven research across different modalities.

3.2.2 Precision Technologies and Digital Image Forensics

In the arts, humanities and social sciences disciplines, diagrammatic representations such as maps, for example, can be used to illustrate features and conditions that take time to explain only in words. This requires precision tools, such as CAD-CAM, vector graphics, and graph generation. At the time of writing this Element, AI technologies have begun to make significant inroads into fields dominated by such precision tools. An example is the combination of Adobe Firefly with Illustrator, particularly through the Firefly Vector Model, enabling the creation of precision vector graphics directly from textual prompts. While generative AI applications in these areas are evolving and not yet ubiquitous, especially in consumer-level products, they are increasingly influencing professional practices. We envision that the continued development and integration of AI in these disciplines could lead to groundbreaking changes, making advanced generative tools more accessible to the general public. Such advancements hold the promise of significantly enhancing the capabilities of diagrams, graphs, maps, and other visual tools, marking an exciting frontier in AI applications.

In the same breath, we additionally see possibilities for other areas of AI and Image. One example that is currently developing and expanding significantly is the field of image/digital forensics. Beyond the fields of arts and cultural heritage, image processing in digital forensics is a contentious issue. In digital forensics proper, several legislative and ethical challenges must be addressed before AI can be broadly implemented. If AI processes images containing personal data, there is a risk of mishandling or misuse of this information. AI could further be employed to generate false or misleading evidence. Another critical challenge is ensuring the transparency and accountability of AI systems. If an AI system makes an error, it should be possible to understand the cause of the mistake and how to prevent similar errors in the future. While AI has the potential to revolutionise digital forensics, these important challenges must be resolved before forensics can be widely adopted (Gupta et al., 2023: 433–447).

Recent scholarship is only beginning to investigate the possibilities for digital image forensics, with a comprehensive review of digital image forensics, focusing on the challenges and advancements in detecting image forgery using AI and machine learning techniques. Some issues that can be highlighted are the increasing ease of image manipulation due to advanced editing tools and the critical need for reliable detection methods to combat misinformation and malicious uses. There exist various image forgery techniques such as copy-move, splicing, retouching, and morphing, and evaluates different machine learning and deep learning approaches for detecting these forgeries. Scholars emphasise the superior performance of deep learning models in identifying forgeries, despite challenges like sophisticated manipulation techniques, rapidly evolving methods, lack of reliable ground truth labels, and privacy concerns. Ongoing research and development of advanced techniques are essential to effectively detect fake images and mitigate the spread of misinformation (see Singh et al., 2024; Spennemann, 2024: 1453–1471).

3.2.3 AI and Its Impact on Our Planet

While we simply do not have the space to expand on this short Element, we hope to raise awareness on how artificial intelligence (AI) has a complex and multifaceted impact on climate change, presenting both opportunities and challenges. On the positive side, AI is being leveraged to combat climate change in various ways. It is used to predict weather patterns, track melting icebergs, and map deforestation, providing valuable data for climate scientists and policymakers. However, the environmental cost of AI remains significant. The training of large AI models consumes substantial amounts of electricity and produces considerable carbon emissions. AI infrastructure, particularly data centres, also contributes to electronic waste production, water consumption, and the demand for critical minerals often mined unsustainably. The indirect environmental impacts of AI are equally concerning. AI applications can inadvertently encourage unsustainable practices (see Crawford, 2021).

Is there light in the end of the tunnel? Perhaps, the United Nations Environment Programme recommends establishing standardized procedures for measuring AI's environmental impact, developing regulations for companies to disclose the environmental consequences of AI-based products, and encouraging the use of renewable energy in data centres (https://www.unep.org/news-and-stories/story/ai-has-environmental-problem-heres-what-world-can-do-about). There is also a push for making AI algorithms more efficient to reduce energy demand and implementing proper waste management systems. The future impact of AI on climate change will largely depend on how it developed and deployed. While AI has the potential to significantly contribute to climate change mitigation and adaptation efforts, it is crucial to manage its own environmental footprint. This requires a holistic approach that considers not just the immediate applications of AI in climate action but also its systemic effects and life-cycle impacts. As AI technology continues to evolve, its relationship with climate change remains dynamic. This necessitates ongoing research, policy development, and collaboration between technologists, environmental scientists, and policymakers to ensure that AI becomes a net positive force in the fight against climate change.

4 Harnessing Machines: Cultural Policy, Participation, and Implementation

4.1 Towards a Regulation of AI in Europe

Disclaimer: none of us authors has training in legal matters, but we have had to deal professionally with some of these issues mentioned below.

4.1.1 Humane AI, Sustainable AI, and the Potential Impact It May Have on the Art and Heritage Sector

This section focuses on legal dialectics and policies that derive from within the European Union and supported by the European Commission which further reinforce and highlight that collaborations require humans and developers of AI systems to work together as partners to ensure integration of learning, reasoning, perception, and interaction in AI development. In this light, AI appears to deliver a complex promise that it will facilitate the work of professionals and the needs of an audience. European art and cultural heritage collections contain historical artefacts that are multifarious, diverse, appropriated, selected, and displayed by contemporary humans, intended for contemporary and future human audiences – including acquiring artefacts as a result of conflict or colonialism (Dunn et al., 2019: 253–271). These systems of interaction between humans, artefacts, and information are deeply contextual, influenced by socio-material factors such as the GLAM legacy, location, the artefacts themselves, and curatorial input (Macdonald, 2011: 81–97). This complexity, and other issues, is precisely what this section aims to problematize, by bringing together and attempting a close reading of different strands of AI Art and Heritage policies, with a focus on current development in the European Union.

Since the beginning of the 2020s, if not, in some cases, earlier, AI has been brought up as a subject of discussion among disparate EU initiatives. The Humane-AI research project, funded by the Horizon Europe scheme of the European commission, is a prime example of these efforts at a transnational level, focusing on the European landscape and publishing a roadmap to assist such processes, considering AI and humanity more generally (https://www.humane-ai.eu/research-roadmap/). By addressing these core challenges, the aim is to develop AI in a sense as assisting technologies to the human condition. On the one hand, the roadmap includes developing AI systems that can understand humans and adapt to complex real-world environments, while respecting human autonomy and self-determination. On the other hand, ensuring AI enhances human capabilities and empowers individuals and society, rather than replacing or dominating humans. In the same breath, humane AI means ensuring a responsible AI. Responsible AI can be translated as a means to addressing the societal implications of AI, such as its impact on employment, inequality, and human rights. Ideally it should incorporate principles of accountability, responsibility, and transparency into the development of AI systems. Additionally it means addressing security and privacy concerns that come with AI and related technologies. This may include ensuring protection of sensitive and personal data used to train AI models, integrating cybersecurity-related courses and knowledge about data protection regulations (e.g. GDPR) into AI education. Bias mitigation is also central to the concept of humane AI, for example, identifying and mitigating biases in AI systems to ensure fairness and inclusivity, improving the accessibility of AI technologies for diverse user groups. Another issue that responsible AI is preoccupied with is transparency, specifically addressing the transparency deficit and trust inadequacy in current AI technologies. Finally, bridging the education gap by integrating human-centred practices, including ethical considerations, into AI education and training programs. To summarise, humane AI challenges revolve around ensuring that AI development in Europe aligns with human values, respects individual rights, and benefits society as a whole.

Armed with a roadmap for humane AI and along the same lines, more precise and specific national initiatives have popped up since then, focusing on the complexity of using AI in the cultural and creative sectors. In April 2022, the presidency of Italy, within the auspices of the European commission, articulated the need to harness AI and its uses in the cultural heritage sector. (https://rm.coe.int/digital-technologies-including-ai-for-cultural-heritage-in-the-framewo/1680a5ea9b). In this context it is recognised that the rapid advancement of new technologies, particularly AI, poses both incredible opportunities and significant challenges for the cultural heritage sector. While AI has the potential to dramatically transform the way we analyse, manage, and protect our shared cultural heritage, its uncontrolled use also raises ethical concerns around bias, marginalisation, and the exacerbation of intolerance and prejudice. In this framework, It was understood that at the time (2022), the Council of Europe conventions on cultural heritage, while recognising the value of digital practices, do not sufficiently emphasise the pivotal role of technological advancements within current heritage practices. It would be beneficial to start a conversation about how to better integrate current heritage practices and to relate them to technological progress within the existing conventions.

4.1.2 The AI Act

Essentially, initiatives as the aforementioned ones have led to the formal establishment of the AI Act. The AI Act was implemented when the European Parliament approved it on March 13, in 2024 with a vote of 523:46 (https://artificialintelligenceact.eu/ai-act-explorer/). It entered into force twenty days after its publication in the Official Journal of the EU, setting the stage for its enforcement and application across the EU. The European AI Act is a ground-breaking legislative proposal, which aims to regulate AI systems in the EU to ensure safety, transparency, and compliance with fundamental rights. There are a number of key points addressed by the AI act, for example, such as scope and classification, provisions, timeline, global impact, enforcement and oversight, compliance, and governance. These are analysed as follows: scope and classification concerns AI systems that are categorised based on risk levels, namely limited risk and high risk. Strict obligations apply to high-risk AI systems due to their potential harm to health, safety, fundamental rights, environment, democracy, and the rule of law. It will become applicable two years after its entry into force, in 2026, with specific provisions taking effect sooner. The AI Act is anticipated to set global standards for AI regulation, influencing other jurisdictions. Organisations using AI systems are advised to develop AI governance strategies aligned with the Act's principles. National competent authorities in each Member State will enforce the AI Act. The Act aims to position the EU as a leader in responsible AI development, emphasising safety, transparency, traceability, non-discrimination, and environmental friendliness. Compliance strategies should align with business objectives and existing legislation. Organisations are encouraged to identify and mitigate risks, establish monitoring mechanisms, and ensure compliance with AI governance standards.

The AI Act represents a significant step towards establishing a comprehensive legal framework for AI regulation in the EU, emphasising the importance of ethical and responsible AI development while fostering innovation and trust in AI technologies. The implications of the AI Act for the creative and heritage industries are significant. The European Union's AI Act introduces a comprehensive framework to regulate artificial intelligence, particularly focusing on generative AI and addressing copyright concerns. The AI Act emphasises the need for responsible AI governance to balance innovation with the protection of fundamental rights, highlighting the importance of transparency in AI systems to ensure accountability and enforcement. Moreover, the Act calls for collaboration and engagement with stakeholders in the creative and heritage sectors to navigate the complexities of AI regulation while fostering a thriving creative ecosystem that respects fundamental rights and addresses challenges related to copyright, authenticity, and authorship of AI-generated content. It also stresses the importance of establishing interoperable digital infrastructures, harmonised digital practices, and capacity building to leverage AI efficiently in studying, safeguarding, and promoting cultural heritage.

4.2 Towards a Legal and Ethical Regulation of AI

4.2.1 AI, Art, Culture, and Creativity (Beyond the European Union)

While not entirely assessed for the art and cultural heritage sector, there are some legal and ethical challenges discussed by other countries and also posed by generative AI, particularly concerning intellectual property (IP) rights. Generative AI, which creates content by analysing vast datasets, is increasingly used in creative industries. However, its use raises significant legal questions about copyright, patent, and trademark infringement. The core issue is whether AI-generated works are considered derivative and unauthorised, potentially violating existing IP laws. The legal landscape is further complicated by the fair use doctrine, which allows limited use of copyrighted material without permission for purposes like criticism, comment, and research. The interpretation of what constitutes transformative use is crucial, as seen in the Google Books case and the pending U.S. Supreme Court case involving the Andy Warhol Foundation (Tang, 2024). To mitigate risks, AI developers are encouraged to ensure compliance with IP laws by properly licensing training data and maintaining transparency about the data's provenance. Businesses using generative AI should include protective clauses in contracts and demand indemnification from AI providers. Content creators should actively monitor for unauthorised use of their works and consider building their own datasets for

AI training. Additionally, many born-digital collections may contain content from multiple copyright holders, often without clear ownership information. GLAM institutions must carefully navigate copyright laws when processing and making such collections accessible using AI. Obtaining necessary permissions or relying on exceptions/limitations in copyright law is crucial. For Europe especially, collections may contain personal information or sensitive data. Institutions must comply with data protection regulations like GDPR to ensure privacy and prevent unauthorised disclosure when using AI.

In the United States, the regulation of AI, particularly in the context of copyright and the art and creative industries, is still evolving. The U.S. Copyright Office has been grappling with the implications of AI-generated works. Current U.S. copyright law requires a minimum degree of human creativity for a work to be protected, which poses challenges for AI-generated content. Japan has been proactive in addressing the intersection of AI and copyright. The Japanese Agency for Cultural Affairs has convened panels to discuss the required threshold for human creative contributions in AI-generated works. Japan's copyright law does not protect the creators of data used for AI training, which creates a grey area for AI-generated content (see Ramalho, 2021). India's approach to AI and copyright is similar to that of the United States. The Indian Copyright Act defines the author of a computer-generated work as the person who causes the work to be created. However, AI-generated works may not meet the creativity requirement necessary for copyright protection if they are seen as mere compilations of existing data without any creative input (Jodha & Bera, 2023: 1737–1748). At the time of writing this Element there is mobilisation towards the Berne Convention for the Protection of Literary and Artistic Works, which has 181 signatory countries, and provides a potential framework for international cooperation on AI and copyright. While the convention is limited by the national laws of its member countries, it can serve as a forum for establishing baseline protections for artists in the context of AI. Additionally, the G7 has launched the Hiroshima AI process to address the global impact of AI, and the OECD has developed AI principles that could influence international standards. These efforts aim to harmonise AI regulations across different jurisdictions, addressing issues such as intellectual property rights and ethical AI use.

Concerning AI and image, there are challenges and considerations to be taken into account more generally. When it comes to art and generative AI, one of the main challenges is ensuring transparency and obtaining consent from artists whose works are used to train AI models. This is crucial for protecting intellectual property rights and ensuring fair compensation. There is a need for ethical guidelines to ensure that AI enhances rather than replaces human creativity.

This includes addressing issues such as deepfakes and the authenticity of AI-generated content. Concerning copyright, two critical policy questions will shape the impact of generative artificial intelligence (AI) on the knowledge economy and the art and creative sector. The first question addresses how we approach the training of these models, specifically whether the creators or owners of the data that are scrapped (lawfully or unlawfully, with or without permission) should be compensated for their use. The second question concerns the ownership of the output generated by AI, which is continually improving in quality and scale. These issues fall within the realm of intellectual property, a legal framework designed to incentivize and reward only human creativity and innovation.

For some years, Britain has maintained a distinct category for computer-generated outputs. On the input issue, the EU and Singapore have recently introduced exceptions allowing for text and data mining or computational data analysis of existing works. The broader implication of these policy choices, weighing the advantages of reducing the cost of content creation and the value of expertise against the potential risk to various careers and sectors of the economy, is that this approach might be deemed unsustainable. Lessons may be found in the music industry, which also went through a period of unrestrained piracy in the early digital era, epitomised by the rise and fall of the file-sharing service Napster. Similar litigation and legislation may help navigate the present uncertainty, along with an emerging market for legitimate models that respect human copyright and are transparent about the provenance of their own creations. (Chesterman, 2025)

Finally, as different countries have varying approaches to AI regulation, this can lead to conflicts and challenges in implementation and enforcement. International cooperation and harmonisation of regulations are essential to create a fair and balanced global framework. As we have tried to briefly show, while the EU has taken a leading role in regulating AI in the cultural and creative sectors, other regions are also developing their own frameworks. The global nature of AI and the Internet necessitates international cooperation to address the complex legal and ethical issues surrounding AI-generated content.

4.2.2 Final Words: AI and Ethical Considerations

Beyond legal considerations alone, institutions ought to take into account additional ethical issues that may arise with the use of AI for image collections. While these may hold no legal gravity, they might be useful to audiences and institutions alike. These include transparency, accountability, human oversight/supervision and collaborative approaches with the community/communities.

Institutions therefore need to be transparent about the data and AI models used, creating detailed documentation (datasheets, model cards) for users and future colleagues or potential partnering stakeholders. Additionally, professionals clearly ought to communicate the capabilities, limitations, and potential biases of the AI system. There needs to be accountability and clear professional roles, responsibilities, and oversight mechanisms for the development and deployment of AI systems. These will ensure accountability for AI decisions and outputs. Last, but certainly not least, professionals and institutions need the professional skills and capacity to be able to examine training data and models for potential biases related to gender, race, ethnicity, or other sensitive attributes. That may involve bias detection and mitigation techniques, as well as involving diverse stakeholders in data annotation and model evaluation. In this sense it is pivotal that there is human supervision, oversight, and intervention over AI systems and not entirely automated decisions, particularly for high-stakes decisions or sensitive collections. This would additionally mean that institutions should not only seek but also actively instigate cross-sector collaborations and knowledge sharing with other institutions, researchers, and technology providers so as to align AI practices with established professional ethics codes and guidelines.

5 Conclusions and Prospects for the Future of AI in Art and Culture

5.1 Now and the Future

5.1.1 What Now?

AI and Image aimed at providing a critical examination of the nexus of AI, art, and cultural heritage, precisely focusing on the promise and the challenges of AI technology applied to images more generally. This Element's primary aim was to demystify AI implementation for images and image datasets. The Element's central purpose is to inform and to discuss the history and the applications of AI to the art and cultural heritage sector and to essentially problematise how such innovative technology may be used in the art and cultural heritage sectors to increase the quality and efficiency of people's work. While AI's inherent capability of autonomy and adaptivity is in itself an asset, we also attempted to flag out the complexities that arise with automation in a world of equally fast developing technology – particularly in Sections 3 and 4.

In conclusion, the implementation of AI in museums and heritage organisations is a diverse and complex yet worthy enterprise, as it encompasses reasoning, classification, knowledge representation, curation, and learning through image processing and analysis. AI's role in curating image collections through automated processes and machine learning is significant, as professionals integrate emerging AI tools to enhance curation, analysis, and dissemination. This integration has transformed the landscape of art and culture, similar to its impact on archaeology. AI and Image critically assess AI's challenges and possibilities in art and heritage studies, aiming to contribute to the discourse on digital transformation in historical disciplines, including the sociopolitical diversity of human memory, the complexity of open access, and funding limitations. We hope that we have emphasised the importance of considering critical perspectives on AI's application to image collections, including the need to understand the ontological and relational qualities embedded in AI technologies. The application of AI in heritage and art always runs the risk of amplifying societal biases; therefore, we believe that institutions and professionals should be reducing bias. Finally, we hope we have shown that the correct approach to AI and image is neither dystopian nor utopian but aims to balance existing societal inequalities through thoughtful implementation in relation to human expertise and diversity.

5.2 Prolegomena to an AI and Image Guide

This Element will not be complete if we did not provide what we consider a best practice approach. In Sections 5.2.1–5.2.5, we envisage this approach, a step-by-step guide should a museum or art gallery desires to implement AI for their image collections:

5.2.1 Identifying the Task

Embarking on the journey of applying specialised AI and machine learning techniques to art and cultural heritage datasets requires a clear focus and a meticulous approach. What do we want at the end of the process? Whose needs should we fulfil? What is to be explained and for whom? Are we curating an exhibition, preparing an online catalogue, or do we want to develop new search tools for the museum sector? One way in shaping the course of action is to consider the dynamic interplay between *primary focal points*, like the object, the audience, and the context. In this way, the task can be described as *audience-driven, context-driven,* or *object-driven*. So, before everything else: Identify the task!

Curators and researchers trained in the humanities do not suppose 'ground truths' as such, as we already have pointed out (see Section 1, Section 1.2.2). It suffices to propose plausible solutions of the tasks at hand, relative to expected outcome. So, determine whether the task is object-driven, audience-driven, or context-driven. Does the primary interest lie in the *object* (e.g. the unique wooden sculpture of St. George in Stockholm, see Figure 14), the *context*

AI and Image 69

Figure 14 St. George and the Dragon, Storkyrkan in Stockholm, inaugurated 1489, by Bernt Notke from Lübeck. Photo: Wikipedia Commons.

(church art within the mediaeval Hanseatic trade area), or with the *audience* (how should we communicate the function of a memorial sculpture to the audience?). This categorisation helps clarify the primary focal point, be it curating collections, fine-honing specialised search machines, catering to specific audiences, or highlighting contextual aspects. As we have pointed out several times, there are no universal guidelines or quick solutions for managing images with AI tools: different approaches and image frameworks are required, varying with the content's complexity and the curator's objectives.

Object-Driven Task: In scenarios where the object takes precedence, such as large catalogues, the focus is on curating collections or specific artefacts. Detailed analysis of materiality (paintings or photographs, for example), historical significance, and pictorial values may become paramount.

Audience-Driven Task: Alternatively, when the audience dictates the approach, considerations may range from catering to schoolchildren with simplified explanations to engaging specialised audiences like amateur or professional researchers with in-depth content.

Context-Driven Task: For tasks propelled by contextual factors, such as historical events or cultural phenomena, the emphasis lies on illuminating significant aspects of the human condition through relevant cultural artefacts.

When the focal point has been established, we need a well-annotated, well-structured, and machine-readable dataset, the digitised collection, to work on.

5.2.2 Data Collection and Preparation

First, audit and prepare your image collection by assessing quantity and quality, ensuring legal compliance, selecting and sorting based on relevance and desired AI applications, converting to suitable formats, and organising with metadata to train AI models. Knowledge of different image frameworks mentioned in Section 1.2.2 is important when making choices, especially for ambivalent image collections bringing up questions on historical bias.

1. Audit the image collection to determine the quantity and quality of images available. A large, well-structured and well-annotated with metadata diverse dataset is crucial for training effective AI models.
2. Ensure ethical as well as legal compliance by reviewing copyright permissions and obtaining necessary releases for any identifiable individuals in the images (see Figure 15 and Section 4.2).

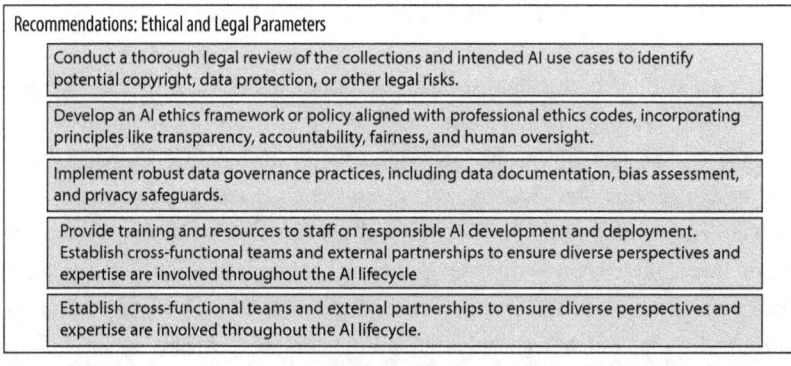

Figure 15 By proactively preparing ethical parameters and addressing legal and ethical concerns, GLAM institutions can leverage the benefits of AI while upholding public trust, professional ethics, and responsible data stewardship. Illustration: J. v. Bonsdorff.

AI and Image   71

3. Select and sort the images based on relevance, subject matter, and desired AI applications. On the object-driven level this would be, for example, object recognition, style transfer, and colourisation. When the context should be made clear, a historical frame (or other research-based frame, cf. the image frameworks, Section 1.2.2) can be delineated and the subject matter can be sorted on different levels.
4. Convert images to appropriate file formats (e.g. JPG, PNG) and ensure consistent aspect ratios and resolutions.
5. Organise and label consistently the images with descriptive metadata, such as subject, style, artist, and date, to facilitate an accurate AI training and analysis.

5.2.3 Data Annotation

Next, annotate the images by manually or automatically labelling or segmenting objects, regions, or features of interest. Please see Figure 16 with annotation guidelines especially suited for images and art – in the figure we paraphrase some suggestions made by Jeffrey Bardzell (Bardzell, 2021).

6. Annotate the images by manually labelling or segmenting objects, regions, or features of interest. This process provides plausible, convincing, and relevant data (if not ground truth – cf. discussion in Section 1.2.2) for supervised learning algorithms.
7. Consider using crowdsourcing platforms or professional annotation services to scale up the annotation process efficiently. This is practical when handling large amounts of unequivocal data. On the downside, preciseness may be lost.
8. Ensure annotation quality by implementing rigorous quality assurance measures and providing clear guidelines to annotators. Human supervision is especially important when working with ambivalent data and questions asking for human discernment. We recommend thinking along the lines of choosing the adequate image framework for the task at hand (see discussion in Section 1.2.2 and Table 1).

5.2.4 Model Training and Deployment

After preparing and annotating the data, choose the appropriate AI models and algorithms based on the desired applications.

9. For example, use convolutional neural networks for object detection or generative adversarial networks or generative AI for image synthesis.

Recommendations for Image Annotations

Take the World Views of Images Seriously: AI tools should be developed and trained to understand different cultural perspectives and world views embedded in images, reflecting a wide array of cultural artefacts.

Exploit the Discursive Conventions and Strengths of Images: AI technologies can help identify and utilise the inherent strengths of images, such as agency, metaphor, and symbolism, for curating exhibitions or educational content.

Describe Rounded, Credible Visual Counterparts Embodying Social Trends, Norms, Behaviours, Styles, Attitudes: AI should analyse images to extract and describe elements that reflect social trends and norms, helping curators understand the evolution of these elements over time.

Describe Pictorial Conventions Staging the Visual Arena: AI can assist in identifying and describing pictorial conventions, understanding the composition, arrangement, and framing within images as well as conventions depicting time, space, and agency.

Describe Pictorial Conventions Playing with Suggestive Ambiguity: Utilising AI to interpret ambiguous images can enhance viewer engagement by sparking curiosity and deeper analysis.

Exploit the Richness of Imaginative, Flowery, and Ornate Descriptions in Natural Language: Using detailed, descriptive text in natural language for annotations can significantly enhance the performance of machine learning models.

Let the Images Show a Complex and Imperfect Social World: AI can help present and interpret images that reflect complex social realities, aiding cultural institutions in addressing sensitive social issues. Seriously: AI tools should be developed and trained to understand different cultural perspectives and world views embedded in images, reflecting a wide array of cultural artefacts.

Figure 16 For the AI to function effectively, well-structured and well-annotated data is paramount. These are some guidelines for enhancing image interpretation and engagement for machine learning. Illustration: J. v. Bonsdorff.

10. Split the annotated dataset into training, validation, and testing sets for model training and evaluation.
11. Train the AI models using the annotated image data and fine-tune the models for optimal performance.
12. Evaluate the trained models on the test set and iterate as needed to improve accuracy and robustness.
13. Deploy the trained AI models in a production environment, such as a web application or mobile app, for end-users to interact with and leverage the AI capabilities.

5.2.5 Implementation and Evaluation

Finally, institutions and professionals ought to continuously evaluate their effectiveness in achieving the intended goals. This involves iterating on model training and data annotation, incorporating feedback, and making necessary adjustments. By following these structured steps and recommendations, cultural heritage institutions can effectively integrate AI into their operations, enhancing their ability to preserve, interpret, and present their collections in innovative and engaging ways. Embracing AI not only aids in the practical aspects of collection management but also opens new avenues for research and public engagement, ensuring that the rich and complex tapestry of human history, art, and culture is accessible to all.

5.3 Famous Last Words

Finally, we reach the end of our journey and this Element. We sincerely hope that our readers will not only take the world of images seriously but also understand that our AI overlords should not and will not take entirely the responsibility for the art and heritage sector. Human oversight in AI automation and image collections is crucial for several reasons. AI systems are often trained on datasets that may contain inherent biases. Without human oversight and human discernment, these biases can be perpetuated and even amplified, leading to unfair or unethical outcomes. Human supervisors can identify and correct these biases, ensuring that AI systems operate in a manner consistent with ethical standards and societal values. AI systems can struggle with understanding context and nuances, which are essential in many decision-making processes. Humans excel at interpreting ambiguous data, understanding cultural and social nuances, and making judgements based on this understanding. This capability is particularly important in areas like customer service and complex decision-making. Human oversight ensures that AI and automation are used ethically and in compliance with regulatory requirements- yet that presupposes that humans themselves do not create biased classifications. This includes addressing issues around privacy, data protection, and the impact on jobs.

Human supervisors can ensure that AI systems align with organisational values and legal standards. Humans play a critical role in monitoring the performance of AI systems, identifying areas for improvement, and refining these tools. They can understand the broader business/industry GLAM context and adapt AI strategies as needed, ensuring that the systems continue to deliver value and meet organisational goals. While AI can drive efficiency, it cannot replace the empathy and perception that humans bring to interactions. Human oversight helps maintain a balance, ensuring that the drive for efficiency does not devalue the importance of human interaction, empathy, and emotional intelligence. Effective human oversight involves understanding the complexities of human-algorithm interactions and the regulatory environment. Policymakers and organisations must ensure that human operators are adequately trained and aware of both the system's and their own biases and limitations. This helps in preventing harms and ensuring meaningful human involvement in decision-making processes. We would like to stress how human oversight is essential in AI automation and image collections to ensure ethical use, manage risks, provide contextual understanding, and maintain a balance between efficiency and human empathy. This discriminating oversight helps in mitigating biases, ensuring compliance, and continuously improving the performance of AI systems. In the introduction of this Element, we emphasised how humans should effectively interact with AI: we have shown how AI can be used in fields where humans work and not the other way around; how humans should adapt to AI-driven environments. Only a human-driven environment brings effective interaction with AI. It cannot be the other way around: the GLAM field we are talking about collects human creations of culture and memory, so humans should be at the heart of every stage in any development of technological tools. It takes two to dance: we emphasise that humans and technology collaborate and co-create in bringing artefacts of human memory and culture to the fore.

Glossary

ChatGPT: An AI language model developed by OpenAI, designed to generate human-like text based on input, facilitating conversations.

Computer vision: A field within artificial intelligence (AI) that focuses on enabling computers to interpret and understand the visual world. This technology involves teaching machines to derive meaningful information from digital images, videos, and other visual inputs, allowing them to make decisions or take actions based on that information.

Deep learning: Deep learning is a type of machine learning that uses complex neural networks with many layers (hence 'deep') – this is crucial for tasks like image and speech recognition.

Digitisation: The conversion of analogue (images) to digital formats.

Digitalisation: The digital management and curation of digital artefacts (images) for example, digital annotation, metadata, classification, and categorisation etc.

Born-Digital datasets/Native digital datasets: Datasets that are entirely created/generated and distributed digitally.

Generative AI: A type of artificial intelligence that creates new content, such as text, images, audio, or video, from data.

GLAM: Galleries, Archives, Libraries and Museums.

H-BIM: Heritage – Building Information Modelling.

Large Language Models: Advanced AI systems trained on vast text data to understand, generate, and predict human-like language

Latent space: A multidimensional vector space representing compressed data, where similar data points are closer together, facilitating efficient AI model development.

Machine Learning: A subset of AI where algorithms learn from data to make predictions or decisions without explicit programming.

Metadata, or metainformation: Data that provides information about other data. There are several distinct types of metadata, including: (1) Descriptive Metadata: provides information about a resource, aiding in its discovery and identification. It includes elements such as the title, abstract, author, and keywords. (2) Structural Metadata: the organization of data containers and indicates how compound objects are assembled. For example, it describes how pages are ordered to form chapters and details the types, versions, relationships, and other characteristics of digital materials. (3) Administrative metadata: includes information that helps manage a resource, such as the resource type, permissions, and details about when and how it was created. (4) Reference Metadata: provides information about the contents and quality of statistical data.

Modality/Multimodality: A specific means of communication, such as linguistic, visual, aural, gestural, or spatial modes. Multimodality involves the use of multiple modes of communication within a single text to create meaning, enhancing the audience's understanding through the interplay of different representational forms.

Natural Language Processing (NLP): An interdisciplinary field that combines computer science, artificial intelligence (AI), and linguistics to enable computers to understand, interpret, and generate human language.

Neural networks: A set of algorithms modelled loosely after the human brain that are designed to recognize patterns.

Open Source AI: Refers to AI systems whose source code, model parameters, datasets, and other components are freely available for anyone to use, modify, and distribute.

Explainable AI: Explainable AI (XAI) refers to artificial intelligence systems designed to provide clear, understandable explanations for their decisions and actions.

References

Angileri, J., Brown, M., Dipalma, J., Ma, Z., & Dancy, C. L. (2019). Ethical Considerations of Facial Classification: Reducing Racial Bias in AI. https://doi.org/10.13140/RG.2.2.28601.11368.

Anglisano, A., Casas, L., Queralt, I., & Di Febo, R. (2022). Supervised Machine Learning Algorithms to Predict Provenance of Archaeological Pottery Fragments. *Sustainability* 14, 11214.

Anichini, F., Banterle, F., Buxeda i Garrigós, J., et al. (2020). Developing the ArchAIDE Application: A Digital Workflow for Identifying, Organising and Sharing Archaeological Pottery Using Automated Image Recognition. *Internet Archaeology* 52.

Anichini, F., Dershowitz, N., Dubbini, N., et al. (2021). The Automatic Recognition of Ceramics from Only One Photo: The ArchAIDE App. *Journal of Archaeological Science: Reports* 36, 102788.

Aoulalay, A., El Makhfi, N., Abounaima, M. C., & Massar, M. (2020). Classification of Moroccan Decorative Patterns Based on Machine Learning Algorithms. In *Proceedings of the 2020 IEEE 2nd International Conference on Electronics, Control, Optimization and Computer Science (ICECOCS), Kenitra, Morocco, 2–3 December 2020*, pp. 1–7.

Argyriou, L., Economou, D., & Bouki, V. (2020). Design Methodology for 360 Immersive Video Applications: The Case Study of a Cultural Heritage Virtual Tour. *Personal and Ubiquitous Computing* 24(6), 843–859.

Argyrou, A., Agapiou, A., Papakonstantinou, A., & Alexakis, D. D. (2023). Comparison of Machine Learning Pixel-Based Classifiers for Detecting Archaeological Ceramics. *Drones* 7, 578.

Arnheim, R. (1954). *Art and Visual Perception: A Psychology of the Creative Eye*. Berkeley: University of California Press.

Arnheim, R. (1969). *Visual Thinking*. Berkeley: University of California Press.

Arnold, T. & Tilton, L. (2019). Distant Viewing: Analyzing Large Visual Corpora. *Digital Scholarship in the Humanities* 34, i3–i16. https://doi.org/10.1093/llc/fqz013.

Assael, Y., Sommerschield, T., Shillingford, B., et al. (2022). Restoring and Attributing Ancient Texts Using Deep Neural Networks. *Nature* 603, 280–283. https://doi.org/10.1038/s41586-022-04448-z.

Atairu, M. (2024). Reimagining Benin Bronzes Using Generative Adversarial Networks. *AI and Society* 39(1), 91–102.

Bachmann, R., Fatih Kar, O., Mizrahi, D., et al. (2024). 4M-21: An Any-to-Any Vision Model for Tens of Tasks and Modalities. arXiv:2406.09406v2.

Bagga, S. & Piper, A. (2020). Measuring the Effects of Bias in Training Data for Literary Classification. In *Proceedings of e 4th Joint SIGHUM Workshop on Computational Linguistics for Cultural Heritage, Social Sciences, Humanities and Literature*, pp. 74–84.

Bahrami, M. & Albadvi, A. (2023). Deep Learning for Identifying Iran's Cultural Heritage Buildings in Need of Conservation Using Image Classification and Grad-CAM. arXiv:2302.14354.

Banerjee, I., Bhimireddy, A. R., Burns, J. L., et al. (2021). Reading Race: AI Recognises Patient's Racial Identity in Medical Images. arXiv preprint arXiv:2107.10356.

Bardzell, J. (2021). Lecture 'Chimeras of Boundless Glamour, Realities of Little Worth' at the KTH Royal Institute of Technology, Stockholm 2021. www.kth.se/en/eecs/kalender/seminars/fff-seminar-chimeras-of-boundless-glamour-realities-of-little-worth-1.1046775?date=2021-02-05&orgdate=2021-01-28&length=1&orglength=338; date of access: 6 January 2025.

Barocas, S., Hardt, M., & Narayanan, A. (2023). *Fairness and Machine Learning: Limitations and Opportunities*. Cambridge, MA: MIT Press.

Barthes, R. (1977). *Image-Music-Text*, trans. Stephen Heath. New York: Hill and Wang.

Barthes, R. (1981). *Camera Lucida: Reflections on Photography*, trans. Richard Howard. New York: Hill and Wang.

Baxandall, M. (1988). *Patterns of Intention: On the Historical Explanation of Pictures*. New Haven: Yale University Press.

Bell, P. (2022). Computer Vision und Visualisierung als didaktische Instrumente in der Kunstgeschichte. In (ed. H. Locher & M. Männig) *Lehrmedien der Kunstgeschichte: Geschichte und Perspektiven kunsthistorischer Medienpraxis*, Berlin: Deutscher Kunstverlag, pp. 384–401. https://doi.org/10.1515/9783422986251.

Bell, P. & Ommer, B. (2016). Visuelle Erschließung: Computer Vision als Arbeits- und Vermittlungstool. In (ed. A. Bienert) *EVA Berlin 2016: Elektronische Medien & Kunst, Kultur und Historie*, Berlin, pp. 67–73.

Belting, H. (1994). *Likeness and Presence: A History of the Image Before the Era of Art*. Chicago: University of Chicago Press.

Belting, H. (2005). *Image, Medium, Body: A New Approach to Iconology*. Chicago: University of Chicago Press.

Belting, H. (2005). Image, Medium, Body: A New Approach to Iconology. *Critical Inquiry* 31, 302–319.

Belting, H. (2011). *An Anthropology of Images: Picture, Medium, Body*. Princeton: Princeton University Press.

Bender, E. M., Gebru, T., McMillan-Major, A., & Shmitchell, S. (2021). On the Dangers of Stochastic Parrots: Can Language Models Be Too Big? In *Proceedings of the 2021 ACM Conference on Fairness, Accountability, and Transparency, Virtual, 3–10 March 2021*, pp. 610–623.

Benford, S., Sundnes Løvlie, A., Ryding, K., et al. (2022, April). Sensitive Pictures: Emotional Interpretation in the Museum. In *CHI Conference on Human Factors in Computing Systems*, pp. 1–16.

Benjamin, R. (2019). *Race after Technology: Abolitionist Tools for the New Jim Code*. London: Polity.

Berry, D. & Dieter, M. (2015). *Postdigital Aesthetics*. London: Springer.

Berryman, J. (2024). Creativity and Style in GAN and AI Art: Some Art-Historical Reflections. *Philosophy & Technology* 37, 61. https://doi.org/10.1007/s13347-024-00746-8.

Bharathi Larsson, Å. (2016). *Colonizing Fever: Race and Media Cultures in Late Nineteenth-Century Sweden*. Lund: Media History.

Bickler, S. H. (2018). Machine Learning Identification and Classification of Historic Ceramics. *Archaeology* 20, 20–32.

Blanke, T., & Prescott, A. (2016). Dealing with Big Data. In (ed. G. Griffin & M. Hayler) *Research Methods for Reading Digital Data in the Digital Humanities*. Edinburgh: Edinburgh University Press, pp. 184–205.

Boehm, G. (2007). *Wie Bilder Sinn erzeugen: Die Macht des Zeigens*. Berlin: Berlin University Press.

Bordoni, L., Mele, F., & Sorgente, A. (eds.) (2016). *Artificial Intelligence for Cultural Heritage*. Cambridge: Cambridge Scholars.

Bredekamp, H. (2010). *Theorie des Bildakts*. Frankfurt: Suhrkamp.

Broca, S. (2010). Lawrence Lessig, Remix: Making Art and Commerce Thrive in the Hybrid Economy. *Quaderni: Communication, Technologies, Pouvoir* 71, 121–123. https://doi.org/10.4000/quaderni.535.

Broussard, M. (2018). *Artificial Unintelligence*. Cambridge, MA: MIT Press .

Buolamwini, J. & Gebru, T. (2018). Gender Shades: Intersectional Accuracy Disparities in Commercial Gender Classification. In *Proceedings of the 1st Conference on Fairness, Accountability and Transparency. Conference on Fairness, Accountability and Transparency*, PMLR, pp. 77–91. https://proceedings.mlr.press/v81/buolamwini18a.html.

Butler, J. (1990). *Gender Trouble: Feminism and the Subversion of Identity*. New York: Routledge.

Butler, J. (1993). *Bodies That Matter: On the Discursive Limits of "Sex"*. New York: Routledge.

References

Cao, J., Zhang, Z., Zhao, A., Cui, H., & Zhang, Q. (2020). Ancient Mural Restoration Based on a Modified Generative Adversarial Network. *Heritage Science* 8, 1–14.

Cardarelli, L. (2022). A Deep Variational Convolutional Autoencoder for Unsupervised Features Extraction of Ceramic Profiles: A Case Study from Central Italy. *Journal of Archaeological Science* 144, 105640.

Caton, K., & Santos, C. A. (2008). Closing the Hermeneutic Circle? Photographic Encounters with the Other. *Annals of Tourism Research 35* (1), 7–26.

Chammas, M., Makhoul, A., Demerjian, J., & Dannaoui, E. (2022). A Deep Learning Based System for Writer Identification in Handwritten Arabic Historical Manuscripts. *Multimedia Tools and Applications* 81, 30769–30784.

Chang, K. K., Cramer, M., Soni, S., & Bamman, D. (2023). Speak, Memory: An Archaeology of Books Known to Chatgpt/gpt-4. arXiv.

Chen, X., Shrivastava, A., & Gupta, A. (2013). NEIL: Extracting Visual Knowledge from Web Data. In *Proceedings of (ICCV) International Conference on Computer Vision*, pp. 1409–1416.

Chesterman, S. (2025). Good Models Borrow, Great Models Steal: Intellectual Property Rights and Generative AI. *Policy and Society, 44*(1), 23–37. https://doi.org/10.1093/polsoc/puae006.

Chetouani, A., Treuillet, S., Exbrayat, M., & Jesset, S. (2020). Classification of Engraved Pottery Sherds Mixing Deep-Learning Features by Compact Bilinear Pooling. *Pattern Recognition Letters* 131, 1–7.

Chun, W. H. K. (2021). *Discriminating Data*. Cambridge, MA: MIT Press.

Ciecko, B. (2020). AI Sees What? The Good, the Bad, and the Ugly of Machine Vision for Museum Collections. In *MW2020: Museums and the Web, 5*(1).

Cintas, C., Lucena, M., Fuertes, J. M., et al. (2020). Automatic Feature Extraction and Classification of Iberian Ceramics Based on Deep Convolutional Networks. *Journal of Cultural Heritage* 41, 106–112.

Crawford, K. (2021). *The Atlas of AI: Power, Politics, and the Planetary Costs of Artificial Intelligence*. New Haven: Yale University Press.

Davis, J. L., Williams, A., & Yang, M. W. (2021). Algorithmic Reparation. *Big Data & Society* 8(2). https://doi.org/10.1177/20539517211044808.

Davis, M. & Hunt, J. (2017). *Visual Communication Design: An Introduction to Design Concepts in Everyday Experience*. London: Bloomsbury.

de Sousa Santos, B. (2018). *The End of the Cognitive Empire: The Coming of Age of Epistemologies of the South*. Durham, NC: Duke University Press.

Dorfer, T. A. (2023.) Ten Years of AI in Review. *Towards Data Science*. https://towardsdatascience.com/ten-years-of-ai-in-review-85decdb2a540.

Dumitrache, A., Inel, O., Timmermans, B., et al. (2021). Empirical Methodology for Crowdsourcing Ground Truth. *Semantic Web* 12(3), 403–421.

Dunn, H. & Bourcier, P. (2020). *Nomenclature for Museum Cataloging: Knowledge Organization.* https://doi.org/10.5771/0943-7444-2020-2-183.

Dunn, S., Earl, G., Foka, A., & Wootton, W. (2019). Spatial Narratives in Museums and Online: The Birth of the Digital Object Itinerary. In (ed. T. Giannini & J. Bowen) *Museums and Digital Culture: New Perspectives and Research, Springer Series on Cultural Computing.* Cham: Springer, pp. 253–271. https://doi.org/10.1007/978-3-319-97457-6_12.

Eco, U. (1976). *A Theory of Semiotics.* Bloomington: Indiana University Press.

Eco, U. (1989). *The Open Work.* Cambridge: Harvard University Press.

Ehrenborg, L. (1956). Vår första konstfilm – 'ett ovärdigt profanerande av konsten'. *Ord och bild,* 65, 223–230.

Elkins, J. (2007). *Visual Literacy.* New York: Routledge.

Emerick, K. (2014). *Conserving and Managing Ancient Monuments: Heritage, Democracy, and Inclusion.* Woodbridge: Boydell & Brewer.

Ernst, W. (2013). *Digital Memory and the Archive.* Minneapolis: University of Minnesota Press .

Fabricius. https://experiments.withgoogle.com/fabricius (accessed on 1 February 2024).

Fahse, T., Huber, V., & van Giffen, B. (2021). Managing Bias in Machine Learning Projects. In (ed. F. Ahlemann, R. Schütte, & S. Stiegllitz) *Innovation through Information Systems: Volume II: A Collection of Latest Research on Technology Issues.* London: Springer, pp. 94–109.

Ferrara, E. (2023). Should ChatGPT Be Biased? Challenges and Risks of Bias in Large Language Models. arXiv:2304.03738.

Foka, A. & Griffin, G. (2024) AI, Cultural Heritage, and Bias: Some Key Queries that Arise from the Use of GenAI. *Heritage* 7, 6125–6136.

Foka, A., Attemark, J., & Wahlberg, F. (2022). Women's Metadata, Semantic Web, Ontologies and AI: Potentials in Critically Enriching Carl Sahlin's Industrial History Collection. In (ed. T. Stylianou-Lambert, A. Heraclidou, & A. Bounia) *Museum Media(ting): Emerging Technologies and Difficult Heritage.* London: Berghahn Books, pp. 65–86. https://doi.org/10.1515/9781800733756-005.

Foka, A., Eklund, L., Løvlie, A. S., & Griffin, G. (2023). Critically Assessing AI/ML for Cultural Heritage: Potentials and Challenges. In (ed. S. Lingren) *Handbook of Critical Studies of Artificial Intelligence.* Cheltenham: Edward Elgar, pp. 815–825.

Fontanella, F., Colace, F., Molinara, M., Di Freca, A. S., & Stanco, F. (2020). Pattern Recognition and Artificial Intelligence Techniques for Cultural Heritage. *Pattern Recognition Letters* 138, 23–29.

Fu, X., Yang, Z, Zeng, Z., Zhang, Y, & Zhou, Q. (2022). Improvement of Oracle Bone Inscription Recognition Accuracy: A Deep Learning Perspective. *ISPRS International Journal of Geo-Information* 11, 45.

Gaber, J. A., Youssef, S. M., & Fathalla, K. M. (2023). The Role of Artificial Intelligence and Machine Learning in Preserving Cultural Heritage and Art Works via Virtual Restoration. *ISPRS Annals of the Photogrammetry, Remote Sensing and Spatial Information Sciences*, 10, 185–190.

Gardenier, J. & Resnik, D. (2002). The Misuse of Statistics: Concepts, Tools, and a Research Agenda. *Accountability in Research: Policies and Quality Assurance* 9(2), 65–74.

Garstki, K. (2020). *Digital Innovations in European Archaeology*. Cambridge: Cambridge University Press.

Giugliano, G. & Laudante, E. (2020) Design as Collaborative Connection between User, Technology and Cultural Context. *IOP Conference Series: Materials Science and Engineering* 949(1), 012010. https://doi.org/10.1088/1757-899X/949/1/012010.

Goldstein, A. J., Harmon, L. D., & Lesk, A. B. (1972). Man-Machine Interaction in Human-Face Identification. *The Bell System Technical Journal* 51(2), 399–427. https://doi.org/10.1002/j.1538-7305.1972.tb01927.x.

Gozalo-Brizuela, R. & Garrido-Merchan, E. C. (2023). ChatGPT Is Not All You Need. A State of the Art Review of Large Generative AI Models. https://doi.org/10.48550/arXiv.2301.04655.

Grandjean, M. (2016). A Social Network Analysis of Twitter: Mapping the Digital Humanities Community. *Cogent Arts & Humanities* 3(1). https://doi.org/10.1080/23311983.2016.1171458.

Griffin, G., Wenneström, E., & Foka, A. (2023). AI and Swedish Heritage Organisations: Challenges and Opportunities. In *AI and Society*. London: Springer, pp. 2359–2372. https://doi.org/10.1007/s00146-023-01689-y.

Gross, N. (2023). What ChatGPT Tells Us about Gender: A Cautionary Tale about Performativity and Gender Biases. *Social Sciences* 12(8): 435. https://doi.org/10.3390/socsci12080435.

Grusin, R. & Bolter, J. D. (1999). *Remediation: Understanding New Media*. Cambridge, MA: MIT Press.

Grusin, R. (2004). Premediation. *Criticism* 46(1), 17–39.

Gualandi, M. L., Gattiglia, G., & Anichini, F. (2021). An Open System for Collection and Automatic Recognition of Pottery through Neural Network Algorithms. *Heritage* 4(1), 140–159

Guidi, T., Python, L., Forasassi, M., et al. (2023). Egyptian Hieroglyphs Segmentation with Convolutional Neural Networks. *Algorithms* 16, 79.

Gupta, R., Mane, M., Bhardwaj, S., et al. (2023). Use of Artificial Intelligence for Image Processing to Aid Digital Forensics: Legislative Challenges. In (ed. B. K. Pandey, D. Pandey, R. Anand, et al.) *Handbook of Research on Thrust Technologies' Effect on Image Processing*. IGI Global, pp. 433–447.

Harrison, R. (2013). *Heritage: Critical Approaches*. Routledge: London.

Hayles, N. K. (2017). *Unthought: The Power of the Cognitive Nonconscious*. Chicago: University of Chicago Press.

He, K., Zhang, X., & Jian Sun, R. (2015). Deep Residual Learning for Image Recognition. https://doi.org/10.48550/arXiv.1512.03385.

Head, C. B., Jasper, P., McConnachie, M., Raftree, L., & Higdon, G. (2023). Large Language Model Applications for Evaluation: Opportunities and Ethical Implications. *New Directions for Evaluation*, 2023(178–179), 33–46. https://doi.org/10.1002/ev.20556.

Huster, A. C. (2013). Assessing Systematic Bias in Museum Collections: A Case Study of Spindle Whorls. *Advances in Archaeological Practice* 1(2), 77–90.

Jabeen, S., Li, X., Amin, M.S., et al. (2023). A Review on Methods and Applications in Multimodal Deep Learning. *ACM Transactions on Multimedia Computing, Communications and Applications*, 19(2s), 1–41.

Jodha, D. & Bera, P. (2023). Copyright Issues in the Era of AI – A Critical Analysis. *Res Militaris* 13(3), 1737–1748.

Johannesson, L. (1991). Bildskapande och seendekultur. *Bild i skolan: Lärarförbundets tidskrift för bildpedagogik* 62(4), 9–14.

Johannesson, L. (1999). Demokratins symbolrum: bild och självbild. In (ed. E. Amnå & L. Johannesson) *Demokratins estetik*. Stockholm: Statens Offentliga Utredningar SOU, pp. 11–42.

Kamran, A. (2023). Decolonizing Artificial Intelligence: Unveiling Biases, Power Dynamics, and Colonial Continuities in AI Systems. *RMS Journal*. https://ssrn.com/abstract=4610643.

Karterouli, K. & Batsaki, Y. (2021). AI and Cultural Heritage Image Collections: Opportunities and Challenges. In *Proceedings of EVA London, AI and the Arts: Artificial Imagination (July 2021)*, pp. 193–198. http://dx.doi.org/10.14236/ewic/EVA2021.33.

Kingma, D. P., Rezende, D. J., Mohamed, S., & Welling, M. (2014). Semi-Supervised Learning with Deep Generative Models. arXiv:1406.5298.

Kizhner, I., Terras, M., Rumyantsev, M., et al. (2021). Digital Cultural Colonialism: Measuring Bias in Aggregated Digitized Content Held in Google Arts and Culture. *Digital Scholarship in the Humanities* 36(3), 607–640.

Kress, G. (2003). *Literacy in the New Media Age*. London: Routledge.
Kress, G. (2010). *Multimodality: A Social Semiotic Approach to Contemporary Communication*. London: Routledge.
Kress, G. & van Leeuwen, T. (2021, third ed.). *Reading Images: The Grammar of Visual Design*. New York: Routledge.
Krig, S. (2016), *Computer Vision Metrics: Survey, Taxonomy and Analysis of Computer Vision, Visual Neuroscience, and Deep Learning*, London: Springer. https://doi.org/10.1007/978-3-319-33762-3.
Krizhevsky, A., Sutskever, I., & Hinton, G. (2012). ImageNet Classification with Deep Convolutional Neural Networks. In *Proceedings of the 25th International Conference on Neural Information Processing Systems (Lake Tahoe, NV, Dec. 2012)*, pp. 1097–1105.
Kuck, K. 2023. Generative Artificial Intelligence: A Double-Edged Sword. In *Proceedings of the 2023 World Engineering Education Forum-Global Engineering Deans Council (WEEF-GEDC), Cape Town, South Africa, 23–27 October 2023*, pp. 1–10.
Küçükdemirci, M. & Sarris, A. (2022). GPR Data Processing and Interpretation Based on Artificial Intelligence Approaches: Future Perspectives for Archaeological Prospection. *Remote Sensing*, 14. MDPI AG.
Kumar, P. & Gupta, V. (2023). Restoration of Damaged Artworks Based on a Generative Adversarial Network. *Multimedia Tools and Applications* 82(26), 40967–40985.
Kuntitan, P. & Chaowalit, O. (2022). Using Deep Learning for the Image Recognition of Motifs on the Center of Sukhothai Ceramics. *Current Journal of Applied Science and Technology* 22, 1–15.
Kwok, A. O. & Koh, S. G. (2021). Deepfake: A Social Construction of Technology Perspective. *Current Issues in Tourism* 24(13), 1798–1802.
Landeschi, G. (2023). AI-Based Approaches in Cultural Heritage: Investigating Archaeological Landscapes in Scandinavian Forestland. In (ed. A. Sudmann, A. Echterhölter, M. Ramsauer, et al.) *Beyond Quantity: Research with Subsymbolic AI*. Bielefeld: Transcript-Verlag, pp. 197–216. https://doi.org/10.1515/9783839467664.
LeCun, Y. & Bengio, Y. (1998). Convolutional Networks for Images, Speech, and Time Series. In (ed. M. E. Arbib) *The Handbook of Brain Theory and Neural Networks*. Cambridge, MA: MIT Press, pp. 255–258.
LeCun, Y., Bengio, Y., & Hinton, G. (2015). Deep Learning. *Nature* 521(7553), 436–444. https://doi.org/10.1038/nature14539.
Lee, D. (2019). Deepfake Salvador Dalí Takes Selfies with Museum Visitors. *The Verge*. https://www.theverge.com/2019/5/10/18540953/salvador-dali-lives-deepfake-museum.

León, R. B., Peña, C. A., & Moreno, G. G. (2023). Advances in the Development of an Algorithm for Parametric Identification of Egyptian Hieroglyphs Using Artificial Vision. *Journal of Advances in Information Technology* 14, 788–795.

Locaputo, A., Portelli, B., Colombi, E., & Serra, G. (2023). Filling the Lacunae in Ancient Latin Inscriptions. In *Proceedings of the CEUR Workshop Proceedings*, *Leipzig, Germany, 20–22 September 2023*, pp. 68–76.

Lockshin, R. A. (2007). Aristotle's and Linnaeus' Classifications of Living Creatures. In (ed. R. A. Lockshin) *The Joy of Science*. Dordrecht: Springer, pp. 55–68. https://doi.org/10.1007/978-1-4020-6099-1_5.

Logan, W. & Wijesuriya, G. (2015). The New Heritage Studies and Education, Training, and Capacity-Building. In (ed. W. Logan, M. N. Craith, & U. Kocke) *A Companion to Heritage Studies*. Malden: John Wiley and Sons, pp. 557–573.

Lucchi, N. (2023). ChatGPT: A Case Study on Copyright Challenges for Generative Artificial Intelligence Systems. *European Journal of Risk Regulation*, *15*(3), 602–624.

Macdonald, S. (ed.) (2011). *A Companion to Museum Studies*. Malden: John Wiley & Sons.

Macken-Horarik, M. (2016). Building a Metalanguage for Interpreting Multimodal Literature: Insights from Systemic Functional Semiotics in Two Case Study Classrooms. *English in Australia* 51(2), 85–99.

Makhortykh, M., Urman, A., & Ulloa, R. (2021). Hey, Google, Is It What the Holocaust Looked Like? *First Monday* [Preprint]. https://doi.org/10.5210/fm.v26i10.11562.

Mallen, K. & Park, E. (2006). Is Digitization Sufficient for Collective Remembering? Access to and Use of Cultural Heritage Collections. *Canadian Journal of Information & Library Sciences* 30(3/4), 201–220.

Mankell, B. (2013). *Bild och materialitet: Om föreställningar, synsätt, material och uttryck i måleri, teckning och fotografi*. Lund: Studentlitteratur.

Manovich, L. (2001). *The Language of New Media*. Cambridge, MA: MIT Press.

Manovich, L. & Arielli, E. (2024). *Artificial Aesthetics*. https://manovich.net/index.php/projects/artificial-aesthetics.

Marchant, J. (2023). AI Reads Text from Ancient Herculaneum Scroll for the First Time. *Nature*. https://www.nature.com/articles/d41586-023-03212-1.

Marie, I. & Qasrawi, H. (2005). Virtual Assembly of Pottery Fragments Using Moiré Surface Profile Measurements. *Journal of Archaeological Science* 32, 1527–1533.

Mayr, O. (1970). The Origins of Feedback Control. *Scientific American* 223(4), 110–118.

Mbalaka, B. (2023). Epistemically Violent Biases in Artificial Intelligence Design: The Case of DALLE-E 2 and Starry AI. *Digital Transformation and Society* 2, 376–402.

McGee, R. W. (2023). Is Chat gpt Biased against Conservatives? An Empirical Study. SSRN https://ssrn.com/abstract=4359405 or http://dx.doi.org/10.2139/ssrn.4359405.

Mitchell, W. J. T. (1986). *Iconology: Image, Text, Ideology.* Chicago: University of Chicago Press.

Mitchell, W. J. T. (1994). *Picture Theory: Essays on Verbal and Visual Representation.* Chicago: University of Chicago Press.

Michelson, A. (2017). A Short History of Visual Literacy: The First Five Decades. *Art Libraries Journal* 42(2), 95–98. https://doi.org/10.1017/alj.2017.10.

Milan, S. & Treré, E. (2019). Big Data from the South (s): Beyond Data Universalism. *Television & New Media, 20*(4), 319–335.

Miller, D. & Haapio-Kirk, L. (2020). Making Things Matter. In (ed. T. Carroll, A. Walford, & S. Walton) *Lineages and Advancements in Material Culture Studies.* London: Routledge, pp. 146-157.

Milligan, I. (2022). *The Transformation of Historical Research in the Digital Age.* Cambridge: Cambridge University Press.

Mishra, M. (2021). Machine Learning Techniques for Structural Health Monitoring of Heritage Buildings: A State-of-the-Art Review and Case Studies. *Journal of Cultural Heritage* 47, 227–245.

Mitchell, M. (2020). *Artificial Intelligence: A Guide for Thinking Humans.* New York: Picador.

Mitchell, W. J. T. (2005). *What Do Pictures Want? The Lives and Loves of Images.* Chicago: The University of Chicago Press.

Morán-Fernández, L., Bólon-Canedo, V., & Alonso-Betanzos, A. (2022.) How Important Is Data Quality? Best Classifiers vs Best Features. *Neurocomputing* 470, 365–375. https://doi.org/10.1016/j.neucom.2021.05.107.

Mordvintsev, A., Olah, C., & Tyka, M. (2015). Inceptionism: Going Deeper into Neural Networks. https://research.google/blog/inceptionism-going-deeper-into-neural-networks.

Murphy, K. P. (2022). *Probabilistic Machine Learning: An Introduction.* Cambridge MA: MIT Press.

Murphy, O. & Villaespesa, E. (2020). *AI: A Museum Planning Toolkit.* London: Goldsmiths, University of London.

Natale, S. (2019). If Software Is Narrative: Joseph Weizenbaum, Artificial Intelligence and the Biographies of ELIZA. *New Media & Society*, *21*(3), 712–728.

Navarro, P., Cintas, C., Lucena, M., et al. (2022). Reconstruction of Iberian Ceramic Potteries Using Generative Adversarial Networks. *Scientific Reports* 12, 10644. https://doi.org/10.1038/s41598-022-14910-7.

Oestreicher, L. & von Bonsdorff, J. (2022). From Visual Forms to Metaphors: Targeting Cultural Competence in Image Analysis. In (ed. K. Berglund, M. L. Mela, & I. Zwart) *Proceedings of the 6th Digital Humanities in the Nordic and Baltic Countries Conference (DHNB 2022)*, 343–351. https://ceur-ws.org/Vol-3232/paper33.pdf.

Offert, F. & Bell, P. (2021). Perceptual Bias and Technical Metapictures: Critical Machine Vision as a Humanities Challenge. *AI & Society* 36(4), 1133–1144.

Ooghe, B., Waasland, H. C., & Moreels, D. (2009). Analysing Selection for Digitisation. *D-Lib Magazine*, *15*(9/10), 1082–9873.

O'Sullivan, S. R. (2023). *The Comic Book as Research Tool: Creative Visual Research for the Social Sciences*. Berlin: Walter de Gruyter GmbH & Co KG.

Ostertag, C., & Beurton-Aimar, M. (2020). Matching Ostraca Fragments Using a Siamese Neural Network. *Pattern Recognition Letters* 131, 336–340.

Panofsky, E. (1955). Iconography and Iconology: An Introduction to the Study of Renaissance Art. In (ed. E. Panofsky) *Meaning in the Visual Arts: Papers In and On Art History*. Garden City: Doubleday [and subsequent editions], pp. 26–54.

Paradis, K. (2023). More than Ones and Zeros: Developing an Intersectional Framework for Artificial Intelligence. *Journal of Information Ethics* 32, 70–83.

Perra, L. (2022). Artificial Intelligence, Administrative Proceeding, Protection and Enhancement of Cultural Property. In *International Conference on Computational Intelligence in Pattern Recognition*. Singapore: Springer Nature Singapore, pp. 685–693.

Pierdicca, R., Paolanti, M., Matrone, F., et al. 2020. Point Cloud Semantic Segmentation Using a Deep Learning Framework for Cultural Heritage. *Remote Sensing*, *12*(6), 1005.

Pierdicca, N., Brogioni, M., Fascetti, F., Ouellette, J. D., & Guerriero, L. (2022). Retrieval of Biogeophysical Parameters from Bistatic Observations of Land at L-Band: A Theoretical Study. *IEEE Transactions on Geoscience and Remote Sensing* 60, 1–17. https://doi.org/10.1109/TGRS.2021.3076051.

Plecher, D. A., Eichhorn, C., Seyam, K. M., Klinker, G. (2020). Arsinoë-Learning Egyptian Hieroglyphs with Augmented Reality and Machine

Learning. In *Proceedings of the 2020 IEEE International Symposium on Mixed and Augmented Reality Adjunct (ISMAR-Adjunct)*, IEEE. Brazil: Recife, pp. 326–332.

Poulopoulos, V. & Wallace, M. (2022). Digital Technologies and the Role of Data in Cultural Heritage: The Past, the Present, and the Future. *Big Data and Cognitive Computing* 6(3), 73.

Prescott, A. & Hughes, L. M. (2018). Why Do We Digitize? The Case for Slow Digitization. *Archive Journal*.

Ramalho, A. (2021). *Intellectual Property Protection for AI-generated Creations: Europe, United States, Australia and Japan*. London: Routledge.

Rettberg, J. W. (2023). *Machine Vision: How Algorithms Are Changing the Way We See the World*. London: John Wiley & Sons.

Risam, R. (2018). Decolonizing the Digital Humanities in Theory and Practice. In (ed. J. Sayers) *The Routledge Companion to Media Studies and Digital Humanities*. London: Routledge, pp. 78–86.

Rogers, R. (2013). *Digital Methods*. Cambridge, MA: MIT Press.

Rose, J. (2022). The AI that Draws What You Type Is Very Racist, Shocking No One. *Vice*. www.vice.com/en/article/wxdawn/the-ai-that-draws-what-you-type-is-very-racist-shocking-no-one.

Rose, S. (2022). *Interpreting Art*. London: UCL Press.

Rosenblatt, F. (1958). The Perceptron: A Probabilistic Model for Information Storage and Organization in the Brain. *Psychological Review* 65(6), 386.

Roueché, C. (2002). AI Minds the Gap and Fills in Missing Greek Inscriptions. *Nature* 603, 235–236.

Roueché, C. (2022). Mind the Gap as AI Guesses at Lost Greek Inscriptions. *Nature*, *603*(7900), 235–236.

Rozado, D. (2023) The Political Biases of ChatGPT. *Social Sciences* 12(3), 148.

Rutinowski, J., Franke, S., Endendyk, J., Dormuth, I., & Pauly, M. (2023). The Self-Perception and Political Biases of ChatGPT. arXiv:2304.07333.

Said, E. W. (1978). *Orientalism*. New York: Random House.

Salazar, N. B. (2012). Tourism Imaginaries: A Conceptual Approach. *Annals of Tourism Research* 39(2), 863–882.

Samoilenko, S. A. & Suvorova, I. (2023). Artificial Intelligence and Deepfakes in Strategic Deception Campaigns: The US and Russian Experiences. In (ed. E. Pashentsev) *The Palgrave Handbook of Malicious Use of AI and Psychological Security*. Cham: Springer International, pp. 507–529.

Sanders, D. H. (2028). Neural Networks, AI, Phone-Based VR, Machine Learning, Computer Vision and the CUNAT Automated Translation App – Not Your Father's Archaeological Toolkit. In *Proceedings of the 2018 3rd Digital Heritage International Congress (DigitalHERITAGE) Held Jointly* with 2018 24th International Conference on Virtual Systems & Multimedia (VSMM 2018), pp. 1–5.

Scheuerman, M. K., Pape, M., & Hanna, A. (2021). Auto-Essentialization: Gender in Automated Facial Analysis as Extended Colonial Project. *Big Data & Society* 8(2). https://doi.org/10.1177/20539517 211053712.

Schreibman, S., Siemens, R., & Unsworth, J. (2008). *A Companion to Digital Humanities*. Hoboken: John Wiley & Sons.

Seaver, N. (2017). Algorithms as Culture: Some Tactics for the Ethnography of Algorithmic Systems. *Big Data & Society* 4(2). https://doi.org/10.1177/2053951717738104.

Sharma, P., Ding, N., Goodman, S., & Soricut, R. (2018). Conceptual Captions: A Cleaned, Hypernymed, Image Alt-text Dataset for Automatic Image Captioning, In *Proceedings of the 56th Annual Meeting of the Association for Computational Linguistics*, pp. 2556–2565.

Sharp, J. P. (2002). Writing Travel/Travelling Writing: Roland Barthes Detours the Orient. *Environment and Planning D: Society and Space* 20(2), 155–166.

Shatford, S. (1986). Analyzing the Subject of a Picture: A Theoretical Approach. *Cataloging & Classification Quarterly* 6(3), 39–42.

Shaus, A., Gerber, Y., Faigenbaum-Golovin, S., et al. (2020). Forensic Document Examination and Algorithmic Handwriting Analysis of Judahite Biblical Period Inscriptions Reveal Significant Literacy Level. *PLoS ONE* 15, e0237962.

Silverman, H., Waterton, E., & Watson, S. (2017). An Introduction to Heritage in Action. In (ed. H. Silverman, E. Waterton, & S. Watson) *Heritage in Action: Making the Past in the Present*. Cham: Springer, pp. 3–18.

Singh, S. & Kumar, R. (2024). Image Forgery Detection: Comprehensive Review of Digital Forensics Approaches. *Journal of Computational Social Science*. 7, 877–915, https://doi.org/10.1007/s42001-024-00265-8.

Smith, L. (2006). *Uses of Heritage*. London : Routledge .

Smith, L., Shackel, P., & Campbell, G. (2012). Introduction: Class Still Matters. In (ed. L. Smith, P. Shackel, & G. Campbell. *Heritage, Labour and the Working Classes*. London: Routledge, pp. 1–16.

Smith, T. J. & Plantzos, D. (eds.) (2018). *A Companion to Greek Art*. London: John Wiley & Sons.

Smits, T. & Wevers, M. (2023). A Multimodal Turn in Digital Humanities: Using Contrastive Machine Learning Models to Explore, Enrich, and Analyze Digital visual Historical Collections. *Digital Scholarship in the Humanities* 38, 1267–1280. https://doi.org/10.1093/llc/fqad008.

Sontag, S. (1977a). *The Image-World*. Thousand Oaks, CA: Sage.

Sontag, S. (1977b). *On Photography*. New York: Farrar, Straus and Giroux.

Sontag, S. (2003). *Regarding the Pain of Others*. New York: Farrar, Straus and Giroux.

Spennemann, D. H. (2024). Will Artificial Intelligence Affect How Cultural Heritage Will Be Managed in the Future? Responses Generated by Four genAI Models. *Heritage* 7(3), 1453–1471.

Spitzer, M. (2004). *Metaphor and Musical Thought*. Chicago: University of Chicago Press.

Springstein, M., Schneider, S., Rahnama, J., et al. (2021). iART: A Search Engine for Art-Historical Images to Support Research in the Humanities, In *MM '21: Proceedings of the 29th ACM International Conference on Multimedia*, pp. 2801–2803. https://doi.org/10.1145/3474085.3478564.

Striphas, T. (2015). Algorithmic Culture. *European Journal of Cultural Studies* 18(4–5), 395–412. https://doi.org/10.1177/1367549415577392.

Tamkin, A., Brundage, M., Clark, J., & Ganguli, D. (2021). Understanding the Capabilities, Limitations, and Societal Impact of Large Language Models. arXiv:2102.02503.

Tang, X. (2024). Art after Warhol. *UCLA Law Review*, 2024, 870–944.

Thiel, S. & Bernhardt, J. C. (ed.) (2023). *AI in Museums: Reflections, Perspectives and Applications*. Leiden: De Gruyter, https://doi.org/10.1515/9783839467107.

Tzouganatou, A. (2018). Can Heritage Bots Thrive? Toward Future Engagement in Cultural Heritage. *Advances in Archaeological Practice* 6(4), 377–383.

Tzouganatou, A. (2021). On Complexity of GLAMs' Digital Ecosystem: APIs as Change Makers for Opening Up Knowledge. In (ed. M. Rauterberg) *Culture and Computing Design Thinking and Cultural Computing*. Cham: Springer International, pp. 348–359.

Unesco (1949). *Films on Art: A Specialized Study, an International Catalogue*. Paris: UNESCO.

van den Heuvel, C. & Zamborlini, V. (2021). Modeling and Visualizing Storylines of Historical Interactions: Kubler's Shape of Time and Rembrandt's Night Watch. In (ed. R. Smiragla & A. Scharnhorst) *Linking Knowledge*, Baden-Baden: Ergon-Verlag, pp. 99–141.

Van Giffen, B., Herhausen, D., & Fahse, T. (2022). Overcoming the Pitfalls and Perils of Algorithms: A Classification of Machine Learning Biases and Mitigation Methods. *Journal of Business Research* 144, 93–106.

von Bonsdorff, J. (2019). Visual Metaphors, Reinforcing Attributes, and Panofsky's Primary Level of Interpretation. In (ed. L. Liepe) *The Locus of Meaning in Medieval Art: Iconography, Iconology, and Interpreting the*

Visual Imagery of the Middle Ages. Kalamazoo: Medieval Institute Publications, pp. 110–127.

Verschoof-Van der Vaart, W. B. & Lambers, K. (2019). Learning to Look at LiDAR: The Use of R-CNN in the Automated Detection of Archaeological Objects in LiDAR Data from the Netherlands. *Journal of Computer Applications in Archaeology* 2(1), 31–40.

Villaespesa, E. & Murphy, O. (2020). The Museums + AI Network – AI: A Museum Planning Toolkit. https://doi.org/10.13140/RG.2.2.33549.90085.

Wagner, A., Matulewska, A., & Le, C. (2021). Protection, Regulation and Identity of Cultural Heritage: From Sign-Meaning to Cultural Mediation. *International Journal for the Semiotics of Law = Revue Internationale de Sémiotique Juridique* 34(3), 601–609. https://doi.org/10.1007/s11196-021-09833-x.

Wasielewski, A. (2023a). *Computational Formalism*. MIT Press.

Wasielewski, A. (2023b). 'Midjourney Can't Count': Questions of Representation and Meaning for Text-to-Image Generators. *The Interdisciplinary Journal of Image Sciences* 37(1), 71–82.

Wasielewski, A. (2023c). Authenticity and the Poor Image in the Age of Deep Learning. *Photographies* 16(2), 191–210.

Wright, M. & Ommer, B. (2021). Image Synthesis as a Method of Knowledge Production in Art History. *International Journal for Digital Art History* 8, 155–159.

Zachariou, M., Dimitriou, N., & Arandjelović, O. (2020). Visual Reconstruction of Ancient Coins Using Cycle-Consistent Generative Adversarial Networks. SCI 2(3), 52.

Zhang, M., Fei, H., & Wang B., et al. (2024). Recognizing Everything from All Modalities at Once: Grounded Multimodal Universal Information Extraction. arXiv:2406.03701v2.

Zhao, X., Wang, L., Zhang, Y., et al. (2024). A Review of Convolutional Neural Networks in Computer Vision. *Artificial Intelligence Review, 57*(4), 1–43.

Acknowledgements

We are deeply grateful to the many individuals and institutions that have supported us in writing this Element. First and foremost, we extend our heartfelt thanks to the Wallenberg Foundation and the Wallenberg Autonomous Systems in Humanities and Society Programme (WASP-HS) for their generous funding of the Project Quantifying Culture: AI and Heritage Collections (MAW 2020.0054), which has largely financed the time and expenses associated with this publication.

We are indebted to the WASP-HS community in Sweden, particularly Gabriele Griffin- the co-PI of Quantifying Culture, Ericka Johnson and Virginia Dignum, and Christofer Edling for their invaluable support and insights. Special thanks go to Anna-Sara Lind, Katja DeVries, Yulia Razmetaeva, and Amanda Lagerkvist at Uppsala University and Ilan Manouach at University of Liège in Belgium for their inspirational discussions, brilliant minds, and significant contributions to AI research. Our informal proofreaders, Anders Hast, Johan Vekselius, Anna Soloveva, and Cornelius Persson, have provided us with enormous support and excellent timely comments throughout this process.

Our editors, Michael Rowlands, Kristian Kristiansen, Priyanka Durai and Sowmya Singaravelu, deserve our sincere gratitude for their meticulous care and guidance throughout the publishing process. We also wish to acknowledge our respective institutions and our dear colleagues at Uppsala University – the Department of Archives, Information Studies and Museum and Cultural heritage Studies (ALM), the Department of Art History, and the Centre for Digital Humanities and Social Sciences (CDHU) – for providing a nurturing environment for our work – and dear supportive colleagues Åse Hedemark and Isto Huvila. We extend our appreciation to the expert research engineers of CDHU, Dalia Ortiz Pablo, Sushruth Badri, and Adam Maen for their technical support and for creating a space that allowed our ideas to flourish beyond our initial conceptions. Last, but not least, support by HumInfra, the Swedish National Research Infrastructure in Digital and Experimental Humanities (Swedish Research Council Infrastructure grant 2022–2028), and InfraVis the National Infrastructure for Scientific Visualisation is gratefully acknowledged (Swedish Research Council grant 2021–00181).

On a personal note, we are profoundly thankful to our life partners, Christer Blomquist and Hanna Källström von Bonsdorff, for their brilliant minds but also their unwavering love, care, and support throughout this journey. Finally, we dedicate this book to our children, whose curiosity and wonder continue to inspire us in our exploration of images today.

Cambridge Elements

Critical Heritage Studies

Kristian Kristiansen
University of Gothenburg

Michael Rowlands
UCL

About the Series
This series focuses on the recently established field of Critical Heritage Studies. Interdisciplinary in character, it brings together contributions from experts working in a range of fields, including cultural management, anthropology, archaeology, politics, and law. The series will include volumes that demonstrate the impact of contemporary theoretical discourses on heritage found throughout the world, raising awareness of the acute relevance of critically analysing and understanding the way heritage is used today to form new futures.

Cambridge Elements

Critical Heritage Studies

Elements in the Series

Global Heritage, Religion, and Secularism
Trinidad Rico

Heritage Making and Migrant Subjects in the Deindustrialising Region of the Latrobe Valley
Alexandra Dellios

Heritage and Design: Ten Portraits from Goa (India)
Pamila Gupta

Heritage, Education and Social Justice
Veysel Apaydin

Geopolitics of Digital Heritage
Natalia Grincheva and Elizabeth Stainforth

Here and Now at Historic Sites: Pupils and Guides Experiencing Heritage
David Ludvigsson, Martin Stolare and Cecilia Trenter

Heritage and Transformation of an African Popular Music
Aghi Bahi

Will Heritage Save Us? Intangible Cultural Heritage and the Sustainable Development Turn
Chiara Bortolotto

The Neoliberalisation of Heritage in Africa
Rachel King

Why Historic Places Matter Emotionally: Responses – Attachments – Communities
Rebecca Madgin

In Search of National Ancestors: Heritage, Identity and Placemaking in China
Shu-Li Wang

AI and Image: Critical Perspectives on the Application of Technology on Art and Cultural Heritage
Anna Foka and Jan von Bonsdorff

A full series listing is available at: www.cambridge.org/CHSE

For EU product safety concerns, contact us at Calle de José Abascal, 56–1°, 28003 Madrid, Spain or eugpsr@cambridge.org.

www.ingramcontent.com/pod-product-compliance
Lightning Source LLC
LaVergne TN
LVHW011849060526
838200LV00054B/4240